OH DEAR, SOMEBODY SAID "LEARNING DISABILITIES"!

A BOOK FOR TEACHERS AND PARENTS

Marnell L. Hayes

Academic Therapy Publications
San Rafael, California
1975

© *Copyright 1975*

Academic Therapy Publications
1539 Fourth Street
San Rafael, California 94901

All rights reserved.
This book,
or parts thereof,
may not be reproduced
in any form
without permission
from the publisher.

International Standard
Book Number: 0-87879-127-2

Library of Congress
Catalog Card Number: 75-24927

First printing: 1975
Second printing: 1976

Illustrations: Marjorie L. Summers

This book was set in IBM
Press Roman 11 point medium
and medium italic type.
Chapter titles were set
in Varityper Univers
24 point and 18 point
light condensed; section headings
were set in IBM Univers 11
point bold. The paper used
was 60 pound Bookwhite for
the text; 10 point CIS for
the cover.

Printed in the
United States of America

Table of Contents

5   Introduction

9   How It Feels To Have A Learning Problem

25   A Simple Approach To The Problem

33   The Auditory Learner

43   The Visual Learner

55   Touch-and-Do Learning

65   Interference: A Special Set Of Problems

73   Individualizing Learning In Groups: Simple Behavior Modification

85   Conclusion

87   Suggested Readings

to

Dr. C., my teacher, my friend

Introduction

Whether taught or untaught, by design or otherwise, all children learn. They learn what we teach them and what we are. They learn from one another and from the very fact that they are alive. Some learn more slowly than others, but still they learn, from the budding Einstein to the profoundly retarded child whose greatest accomplishment may be learning to reach his mouth with a spoon.

Beyond the differences in learning ability which are caused by intelligence, environment, and opportunity, there are still unexplored differences in the ways children learn which may have a profound effect upon the quality of their learning. Despite the sophistication of intelligence testing and awareness of cultural and experiential influences upon the learning of children, we may still be dealing with only the surface of a complex set of interrelated factors, the knowledge of which, when fully explored, may contribute immeasurably to the education of all children.

In the process of teacher training, we have traditionally spent a great deal of time on what children must learn and how to teach them, with relatively little emphasis on how they learn. We introduce teacher trainees to the concept of individual differences in terms of relatively gross distinctions, but rarely to the idea that two children may be equally capable but may approach learning in totally different ways. That is, we stress *content,* and neglect *process*.

As we deal with the abilities of learners, we notice first the marked distinctions: the severely handicapped, and the clearly capable child. Later we begin to make finer and finer distinctions, until we have differentiated the profoundly handicapped, the superior, and a dozen gradations between. In so doing, we come to recognize that categorization is difficult and often unfair, for as we recognize slight differences over a number of variables, it becomes clear that we are dealing in reality with more than a single continuum of abilities.

Over the years, as we have begun to recognize the continuum from profound handicap to pronounced superiority, we have also found that the lessons we have learned in the development of methods and materials for the education of the deviant child can help us teach those children nearer the center of the continuum.

Similarly, as we have recognized many kinds of special needs in children, we have sought to devise special ways of meeting those needs. New teaching methods and materials have been developed to help children whose disabilities could be clearly diagnosed. Braille instruction and mobility training have extended the horizons for the blind child, and many of the methods and materials developed for use with the severely visually limited child are now used for the child with mild visual problems. Some of the principles originated in the education of the blind are applied to the education of all children. We have learned, for example, that the concept of "sight-saving" was erroneous: Vision is not a commodity which can be "used up," and the visually handicapped child is better served by using what little vision he may have constantly as an aid in his education. Even a lesson as simple as the best color for "black" boards came from work with the visually handicapped: Black isn't the "best" color at all, for it produces too much glare. Now we call them "chalkboards," and their best color is green.

The puzzle of learning disabilities was unheard of only a few years ago, yet we can be sure that all the teachers who ever taught in a one-room school met children who seemed bright but who had trouble learning. Even in our sophisticated, modern world, we still have questions and argue over definitions in cases of children whose difficulty is painfully evident to all: the children who are clearly bright and motivated, but who have problems with some kinds of academic tasks.

Our state of ineptness troubles all of us, yet we cannot call a moratorium in teacher training while we explore further and let the all-too-few experts train new teacher-educators, as one noted professor of special education has suggested. The children cannot wait. Their time for learning is now.

This book is intended to explore some of the things we have learned about children with learning disabilities, and to apply some of these lessons to the education of normal children and children who differ in their learning patterns in somewhat lesser degrees: Those who cannot be said to have learning disabilities, but who have learning *differences*. It is a book for parents, as well as for teachers in regular and special classrooms. Some of its lessons are to be learned by experience, as the child learns them.

I have avoided, insofar as possible, adding to the "dictionary pollution" we are constantly faced with in the field of education. It is my hope that everything in this book will be comprehensible without the use of a glossary or dictionary, and I have avoided painstakingly the invention of new terms. I cannot, however, avoid the use of the term *learning difference*; but I feel its meaning is clear in context.

The first chapter is intended as both fun and frustration. It is perhaps best learned by a group, with a leader well equipped with the materials from the chapter reproduced by photocopy. The "games" in the chapter are not really games at all, but attempts to simulate the world as the child with divergent learning patterns may very well see it. The reader who seeks to learn these lessons on his own would be well advised to go through, page at a time, avoiding if he can any "peeking ahead" to the next game. Some of the games will be fun. Some will create frustration. Those who experience the games in groups will have a lesson not possible on an individual basis: the opportunity to see individual differences in action. One group member may be able to handle the pencil-and-paper task, but be at a total loss in one of the reading lessons. Others may find all the games painfully difficult. Precious few will find them all a breeze.

The suggestions in the later chapters have been made as practical as possible, with the full knowledge that many teachers, parents, and consultants will not have access to resource personnel and special materials, though sources for such material, as well as for organizations interested in learning disabilities, are given. Some of the suggestions are intended for the children themselves, in an awareness that some children may be seen for extensive and excellent diagnostic work, only to return to a school setting where personnel are neither aware of nor interested in the problems of learning disabilities and learning differences.

Much of what I have said, I have learned from students of all ages. My conviction that we can and must teach the child strategies to deal with his problems began with my observations of Cheri, who quite unconsciously found ways to tune into learning by circumventing certain of her problems at the age of seven. Cathy taught me that some of the behavioral concomitants of a learning disability prohibited dressing such children in distracting clothing which hindered their movements, including dresses with sashes which were doomed to disaster! Doug taught me some easier ways of communicating self-help ideas to children, such suggestions as "out loud inside your head" and "copy it down off the picture in your mind" being sometimes confusing to some adults, but often totally clear to children. The parents of learning-disabled children have taught me, too. My judgment is clearly monitored by their continued valid insistence that we tie theory to reality, and that we teach their children at least as much as we attempt to "cure" them. My university students have taught me much as well, by their questions, their responsiveness, and their own work with children.

                              Marnell L. Hayes, EdD
                              Assistant Professor
                              Texas Woman's University
                              Denton, Texas

Chapter 1

How It Feels To Have A Learning Problem

The infant learns by processing and organizing the many bits of information he gains from his environment by the use of his senses. Each bit of information he sees, hears, feels, tastes, or smells in this way becomes a minute part of his experience, and each bit influences his responses to other bits. He orders and remembers parts of the information, with facts becoming linked by repeated, changing exposures, and by his behavior following exposures. He moves, and he learns from his own movements. Eventually, what he has learned enables him to control his movements rather than simply to observe them. He grows and matures to more and more complex forms of movement, learning to walk, to run, and to climb.

Simultaneously, the child has been hearing sounds and making sounds of his own as he organizes these experiences, until he is able to learn the symbolic sounds of language.

All of these processes—the sensations and perceptions, organization, memory, order, movement, and the use of language—have become a part of the child's pattern of learning.

For some children, however, the pattern does not develop so smoothly. For whatever reason, be it possible brain damage or some undetectable chemical imbalance, the child's processing system may receive mixed or inaccurate messages from the outside world; or his organizing system may be faulty so that transfer and integration from visual (seeing) to auditory (hearing) or tactile (touching) patterns is disrupted; or he may receive and process data correctly but have difficulty in responding by movement, speech, or writing. If the child's problem passes a number of exclusion tests—that is, if it is thought not to be caused by mental retardation, physical handicap, hearing or visual impairment, emotional disturbance, or cultural deprivation—he is said to have a specific learning disability.

Although there is a carefully included exclusion clause in almost all widely accepted definitions of learning disabilities, we need to recognize that, within the learning patterns of a great many children (whether gifted, normal, or those covered by "exclusion clauses") there are some channels better suited to use as channels of learning than others. Indeed, this is true in ourselves as adults as well.

Consider, for example, your own method of remembering the name of a person you have met for the first time. Ask five people to tell you their "best ways" to remember names, and the chances are good that you will receive at least three different answers. One person associates the name with someone he knows by the same first or last name. Another used the name at least three times in conversation to lock it into his memory. Others may need to write it down, or to visualize the name, perhaps asking how it is spelled as an aid to this visualization. And some may simply claim they just never remember names at all until they've known the person for months!

The children whose learning patterns do not provide them an equally accessible learning route through all modalities, but whose learning patterns are not necessarily defective, are the children I refer to as having *learning differences.*

For example, a normal child who had a hearing loss for some years may have come to utilize primarily visual and tactile-kinesthetic modes of learning. Even if the hearing defect is corrected, the child has become used to experiencing learning through other channels, and will therefore have a difference in learning patterns, whether by habit, improvement by constant use, or by clear preference. Awareness of this fact by parent, teacher, and child can serve to make learning more enjoyable and effective. The child can learn to use strong channels for learning where speed and efficiency are critical, and can learn to strengthen the weaker channels.

Although the mentally retarded child's abilities may all be functioning at lowered rates so that all learning channels are impaired according to the degree of retardation, some channels may be more efficient than others. When we recognize that the educable retarded child's rate of learning is approximately one-half to three-fourths that of the normal child, it is clear that we must make every effort to teach the child as effectively as possible in order to help him reach the goal of independence at adulthood. Using his best learning channels can avoid wasting the child's learning years.

Even the gifted child, in whom all learning channels may function at an above-average rate, may have a learning difference in that one channel may be more effective than another. While knowledge of the best channel is hardly as crucial a matter in this case, as it would be in the case of the child whose problem is so severe as to be classified as a learning disability, it is still information useful to our goal of educating all children to their own fullest potential.

It is possible that many teachers, given a wide range of teaching methods from which to choose, will unconsciously choose methods most closely aligned with their own most efficient learning channels. Perhaps the teachers best able to be flexible in their approach and to use varied methods depending upon the needs of the children are the teachers whose learning channels are equally intact, or the teacher willing to explore more closely the way the child views the learning tasks.

The frustration of discrepancy—understanding but being unable to do—may be the most significant aspect of the learning-disabled child's daily life. Learning-disabled children are aware that they have problems. Each learning-disabled child has gone through a serious self-study; and most come up with the same answer: "I am stupid." Those who work with these children may on rare occasions be able to discuss this early self-diagnosis with the child, though that is seldom possible until the child has some better feelings about himself. One may find that the child has consciously gone through complex, secret machinations to prevent his parents from knowing that they have a "stupid child."

How devastating a burden it must be, to be eight or nine years old, and already a failure! Though we can understand and deal with these reactions in the children to a certain extent, too few of us can ever know the extreme impact of the child's disability.

The following series of exercises is designed to simulate a learning disability. You will be asked to do a number of simple tasks, not too different from the child's school tasks, but with one or two added elements which should give you the feeling of having a learning disability.

These activities are based on those I have developed for my most popular teacher and parent workshop, which I call "Try a Learning Disability on for Size." While I'm vain enough to believe that no one can lead this workshop quite as well as I can, I have decided to make these materials available to those who'd like to try! I'll still be traveling around the country with my version of this workshop, in which I have these materials reproduced as "Dr. Hayes' Handy-Dandy Learning Disability Workbook"; but perhaps by publishing this information here, I can reach parents and teachers I might otherwise never meet.

The ideal setting for these activities would be in a group with only one person familiar with the materials. These simulations have been used successfully for groups from ten to three hundred; but a group of fifty or so is ideal, if you have a strong leader. A valuable part of the experience is the experience of difficulty or failure on a simple task, in front of friends or strangers.

To get the most from this experience, you must actually perform each task. You should try not to look ahead until you have completed each activity in turn.

The first activity is a simple drawing exercise. Get paper and pencil ready. Look at Figure A for a few seconds. Look carefully. Now, without looking back at the figure, draw it from memory.

Figure A

Compare your drawing with the stimulus figure. Do the lines curve properly? Is the figure evenly divided into three parts? Are the barbs at the ends of each curved line made up of short, straight lines?

Reproducing this simple, though unfamiliar figure from memory is a task similar to that which the child faces frequently. Yet we make errors in visual memory on this task which we would not accept from children! In groups as small as 25 college-educated (hence, above-average) adults, I frequently find one or more subjects who reproduce this design with four, rather than three, curved lines. With such deviance in above-average adults, perhaps we can be more tolerant of differences in children who range from below average to superior.

Perhaps you feel your drawing is fairly accurate. Whether it is or not, let's try a tracing exercise (a rather frequent remedial tactic); but let's add a "learning disability." If you have tracing paper or onionskin copy paper, use a piece to trace the design accurately, or simply do the best freehand drawing you can muster. Now cover your drawing with another piece of tracing paper, and set up a mirror (a make-up mirror on a stand is best) as shown in Figure B. Have someone hold a cardboard screen be-

Figure B

tween you and your worksheet so that you can see your work only in the mirror. Now trace your design. (If you have no tracing paper, just use a different colored pencil and attempt to retrace your drawing.) Easy does it! No quitting until the drawing is completed—remember, the learning-disabled child can't "turn off" his disability. When your drawing is completed, carefully print (don't write) your name in the upper, right-hand corner of your paper, still looking in the mirror.

If you arranged to do this task in a group, you have probably observed several things: Often, the subject clenches the pencil until knuckles are white. Some subjects (my audiences begin to refer to themselves as "victims" about now!) can't seem to remember how to hold the pencil properly. Those who try this with a ball-point pen may find that a bad writing angle results in no ink flowing. Nervousness may cause the palms to perspire, and the drawing may very much resemble a worksheet a child has carried for three days in a shirt pocket! Not uncommonly, subjects will blame the pencil, or the lighting, or the person holding the cardboard screen—using all the excuses learning-disabled children use! Observation of a group of mirror tracings usually shows tracings by women and generally superior to those by men. Perhaps this is a close-to-home reminder that our learning disability classes are two-to-one male. The suggestion that women are superior in the mirror task because they spend more time looking in mirrors is of doubtful validity—compare drawings made by a man who shaves twice a day!

Let's move from writing to a child's-eye view of reading.

As adults, we have long since forgotten how similar many of the letters look. To a child, each of the following letters, in the type of the preprimer or in the teacher's tidy chalkboard manuscript, may look just the same:

b   d   p   q   g

And each may resemble nothing more than a "stick with a bump on it." The child has learned that a chair is a chair, whether right side up, upside down, whether on this side of the table or that. Now we expect him to learn that what's true of chairs may *not* be true of *b*'s and *d*'s!

15

We know that many learning-disabled children have trouble with left-to-right progression, yet all too often reading readiness materials are presented in first grade only for a brief, set period of time, as though a sense of left-to-right progression were inborn, and needed, at most, only a brief review. Also, we may forget how similar some letters are when they are unfamiliar. Anyone who has tried to learn Morse code, a flag code, or the manual alphabet knows this fact only too well!

Since, you, as an adult, are already so familiar with left-to-right progression that you may be unable to remember when it was new and difficult, we'll try reading right-to-left, with the added hurdle of a few problems with stick-and-bump letters. Read the paragraph in Figure C aloud (if in a group, call on individuals at random to read aloud one sentence each).

Figure C

Once, many years ago, a fiddler came to the village. He stood in the village square and played and sang until the people came to listen and to dance. A jolly butcher danced with the milkmaid. A small boy skipped through the crowd, with his dog nipping at his heels and yapping loudly.

After the fiddler stopped, the people tossed coins into his hat, and brought him milk and cookies for his trouble. It had been a long, weary day, and the fiddler was glad of a rest in this pleasant village.

Now get ready to take a test on that material—don't look back! Simply list all the characters, animal or human, mentioned in the story.

How many did you remember? There should have been five:

- fiddler
- butcher
- milkmaid
- boy
- dog

If a group of people is working on this project at the same time, you have the opportunity to observe several interesting phenomena: Some will not have been able to remember all the characters. Some will list characters not in the story, but who stayed in their memory from someone's reading error. Frequently, someone will misread the reversed "fiddler" as "rabbit," and later that rabbit will appear on someone's list!

Why do above-average adults have trouble remembering five simple items from elementary-level material? Consider a number of factors influencing that reading experience: First, there was tension and pressure produced by knowing you were having trouble reading otherwise simple material. You read one word, blurted it out, and promptly forgot it in your struggle to identify the next word. Your reading style was far from flowing and expressive, hence hardly conducive to good comprehension beyond individual words. If you experienced this simulation with a group, check for other reactions, too: How many were anxiously reading ahead, trying desperately to figure out the next sentence for fear of being called on to read? How many could read silently fairly well, even "prompting" the designated reader, but "froze up" when faced with reading aloud?

Now let's consider some other problems children may face in reading. We observe some children having trouble staying on the right line, often losing their places. Frequently they seem unable to determine where one word stops and another begins. When we consider how slight the difference in "little spaces" between letters, and "big spaces" between words; and then consider that we are asking six-year-old eyes to make accurate discriminations of such slight differences! Look, too, at the possibility of "tailed" letters like *y* and *g* leading the child's eyes off the proper line and on to the line below.

Let's see what reading is like when a few letters look similar, when big and little spaces are confused, and when it's hard to stay on the proper line. Read aloud from Figure D, next page.

This time we won't add a quiz over the material. Examine some of the same influences you noted on the last reading segment, and check for an additional factor: Were you using your finger as a guide? Many teachers prohibit children from using their fingers in this way: yet it is so normal and natural a function that these same teachers, exposed to this reading simulation, are startled to find themselves breaking their own rules!

Figure D

```
       Do  you  rememd ert h e story of      the  three
dilly boats bruff? Ther ewa sa gib dill ydo at,     a
 mibb1 esizeb gill ygoat  , an b a littl e one.
When th eywan ted some nicegr ee rass, th ey
would walk acrosse th dribib ge ng   to a field where
the bra sswas ta llan bgreen. But   Y ut buess
wh oliv eb ung erth edri bge!  es, it was a
troll.
```

Now let's consider the problems faced by a child with one clearly stronger learning channel, who must function in a classroom where assignments are often in his weak channel.

The next simulation is a *silent* reading assignment. You are to read the material in Figure E silently, with none of it to be read aloud. (In groups, the leader should have the participants signal when—and if—the material begins to "come clear" to them.)

Figure E

LADLE RAT ROTTEN HUT

(Heresy ladle furry starry toiling udder warts—warts welcher altar girdle deferent firmer once inner regional verging)

Wants pawn term dare worsted ladle gull hoe lift wetter murder inner ladle cordage honor itch offer lodge, dock, florist. Disk ladle gull orphan worry putty ladle rat cluck wetter ladle rat hut, an fur disk raisin pimple colder Ladle Rat Rotten Hut.

Wan moaning Ladle Rat Rotten Hut's murder colder inset, "Ladle Rat Rotten Hut, heresy ladle basking winsome burden barter an shirker cockles. Tick disk ladle basking tutor cordage offer groin-murder hoe lifts honor udder site offer florist. Shaker lake! Dun stopper laundry wrote! Dun stopper peck floors! Dun daily-doily inner florist, an yonder nor sorghum stenches, dun stopper torque wet strainers!"

"Hoe-cake, murder," resplendent Ladle Rat Rotten Hut, an tickle ladle basking an stuttered oft.

Honor wrote tutor cordage offer groin-murder, Ladle Rat Rotten Hut mitten anomalous woof.

"Wail, wail, wail!" set disk wicket woof, "Evanescent Ladle Rat Rotten Hut! Wares are putty ladle gull goring wizard ladle basking?"

"Armor goring tumor groin-murder's," reprisal ladle gull. "Grammar's seeking bet. Armor ticking arson burden barter an shirker cockles."

"O hoe! Heifer gnats woke," setter wicket woof, butter taught tomb shelf, "Oil tickle shirt court tutor cordage offer groin-murder. Oil ketchup wetter letter, an den—O bore!"

Soda wicket woof tucker shirt court, an whinny retched a cordage offer groin-murder, picked inner windrow, an sore debtor pore oil worming worse lion inner bet. Inner flesh, disk abdominal woof lipped honor bet, paunched honor pore oil worming, an garbled erupt. Den disk ratchet ammonol pot honor groin-murder's nut cup an gnat-gun, any curdled ope inner bet.

Inner ladle wile, Ladle Rat Rotten Hut a raft attar cordage, an ranker dough ball. "Comb ink, sweat hard," setter wicket woof, disgracing is verse.

Ladle Rat Rotten Hut entity bet rum, an stud buyer groin-murder's bet.

"O Grammar!" crater ladle gull historically, "Water bag icer gut! A nervous sausage bag ice!"

"Battered lucky chew whiff, sweat hard," setter bloat-Thursday woof, wetter wicket small honors phase.

O, Grammar, water bag noise!" A nervous sore suture anomalous prognosis!"

"Battered small your whiff, doling," whiskered dole woof, ants mouse worse waddling.

"O Grammar, water bag mouser gut! A nervous sore suture bag mouse!"

Daze worry on-forger-nut ladle gull's lest warts. Oil offer sodden, caking offer carvers an sprinkling otter bet, disk hoard-hoarded woof lipped own pore Ladle Rat Rotten Hut an garbled erupt.

MURAL: Yonder nor sorghum stenches shut ladle gulls stopper torque wet strainers.*

Were you able to comprehend the story? All the words used are fairly common English words, but none were used with any visual meaning: The words were chosen because, in combination, they sound something like the words for which meaning is intended. Clearly, then, the only way to unravel the story is to read it aloud. Go back to Figure E and see how much more content you derive.

What you experienced in reading this story is what is experienced by the child who learns well what he *hears*, but not what he *sees*. Faced with visual learning, such as silent reading assignments, he gets little, if any, content. Permitted to complete the same assignment in an auditory fashion, such as simply reading it aloud, will result in a dramatic difference. All of us have had the frustrating experience of trying to read a letter or newspaper with some sort of distraction, reaching finally the point where we

---

*Howard L. Chace, *Anguish Languish* (Englewood Cliffs, New Jersey: Prentice-Hall, 1956): 19-22. Copyright 1953 by Howard L. Chace; authorized version used by the author's permission.

realize we've read a single paragraph three times without a single word of content "registering."

The learning problems you have been experiencing have been primarily problems of input—getting the information in so that you could process and make sense of it. There are other problems, too, more difficult to simulate. Problems in processing may be simulated by trying to read technical material in a field not your own, perhaps, or simply by having to do complex calculations in your head. Output problems—expression by word or action of what you have learned—are difficult to simulate, too. One interesting simulation of problems in verbal output is possible if you have access to a reel-to-reel tape recorder with three record-playback heads (the type which permits you to monitor from the tape.) For this simulation, equip the recorder with microphones and head phones. Set the machine on "record" and "tape monitor." Set the volume fairly loud, and speak close into the microphone.

This set-up produces "delayed auditory feedback"; that is, what plays into the earphones is what was recorded a fraction of a second previously. The speaker cannot monitor his own speech while he speaks, as he normally does, but only when it is too late to change his intonation or pronunciation. While the simulation may have little or no close parallel to actual learning disability, perhaps the emotional content of the experience is not unlike what is faced by the child with an expressive language problem; perhaps that of the stutterer; or that of the adult stroke victim. The difficulty in maintaining varied tone may be limited. In this simulation, as with all the others, there is a wide difference in the ability to cope with delayed feedback, providing another glimpse of individual differences in above-average groups.

Another good tape trick involves recording two different familiar songs, one on each stereo track. Then play back both at once through headphones. The "victim" should try to sing along, on key, with either song. Perhaps this may give a feel for the distracting influences the distractible learning-disabled child faces when he tries to respond in the "open" classroom.

In these simulations, I have attempted to provide experiences which produce emotional reactions like those we **observe in children** with learning problems. In groups, one observes a multitude of reactions typical of the children's reactions. Participants avoid eye contact with the leader when it is time to select a new reader. They read ahead, trying to master the one sentence they may be called to read. They look ahead at the next exercise; they look at one another's papers; they fidget, squirm, blush, perspire, complain about the quality of print or pencil or paper. Some let out involuntary emphatic expressions, often with four letters! Some find, with some dismay, an onrush of tears. The saving grace, however, is one the children do not have: When the "games" are over, your learning is once again intact. Throughout the simulations, you knew that in a little while, you'd be able to function in your usual manner.

Don't forget the feelings you have experienced in these simulations. Remember them when you become impatient or frustrated with a child. Use them to help you understand the child's reactions, and to help you see the need for alternatives. If you think you're forgetting, get out your mirror design, and put it where we, as parents, often display our children's efforts—taped to the refrigerator door!

At one parent group meeting where this material was presented, parents wore name tags written in school for them by their children. One father, who had seemed early in the evening somewhat resentful at having been "dragged out" to this school meeting, and who had carefully avoided participation, came up during the refreshment period to try the mirror-tracing task. His frustration and ineptness were painfully obvious. His finished product resembled nothing more than it did the smudged name tag his son had labored over that day in school. Told to put the drawing up on the refrigerator as a reminder of what his child went through, and to help him develop patience with his son, the father stood for a long time looking at his work, shaking his head and murmuring: "Don't yell at Larry. Don't yell at Larry."

On another occasion, a father, whose reaction had initially been far more hostile, looked at his mirror-written name on his paper, which slanted down the side where he had run out of space, and reported in a choked voice: "That's just like it looks when my boy writes his name. I don't know how many times I've yelled at him for not knowing how much room his name takes."

One concerned mother watched her husband struggle with aching hand through the mirror tracing, and listened aghast at the "teacher's" comments: "Well, you seem to be having trouble with that. Everyone else only has to do one page. You need practice, so you can stay after school and do extra!" Suddenly the mother found her eyes full of tears as she said, "My God—That's just what we do to Warren every afternoon after school!"

Just remember: Don't yell at Larry.

"DON'T YELL AT LARRY. DON'T YELL AT LARRY."

Chapter 2

A Simple Approach To The Problem

In order to fulfill our responsibilities to the learning disabled child, we need a method to keep before us consideration of the child's overall learning pattern, including both his relative strengths and weaknesses. We need to be able to plot for each child a learning channel from which he can anticipate maximum success, and at the same time, to pinpoint those weak areas which may require remediation. In addition to providing academic material at the appropriate grade level for individualization, we can prescribe the best methods for approaching the material.

Rather than considering the complex theoretical models of learning which exist, let us explore a very elementary, but extremely useful model, which can help in our consideration of appropriate planning for children.

Input

In order to learn, the child must first get information into his system. This **obviously** involves the senses: The child either **sees, or hears,** tastes, or smells something; or he touches or does something. Often, more than one sense is involved at the same time. These five sensory reception areas make up the child's input system. Two factors are necessary in each sense: First, **simple acuity,** or receiving the information completely and strongly enough; second, perception, or being able to receive the information accurately and with meaning. The hard-of-hearing child may receive auditory information weakly, but may be able to receive with full meaning and without distortion. Another child may receive auditory signals full strength, but derive defective or distorted messages from those signals.

A further differentiation necessary in some channels the distinction between *symbolic* messages and *concrete* ones. A large object placed in a child's path is a visual block by its very existence; the written word has visual meaning only because over the years we have consistently given it a particular meaning. A child labeled *dyslexic* may very well see, perceive, and avoid the block in his path, but perceive nothing other than "marks on paper" as the meaning of the written word.

Similarly, a child may be able to interpret quite well the meanings of many environmental sounds, but have difficulty interpreting the spoken word: He may not move out of the street when his mother calls to him to do so, but may do so when he hears and interprets the sounds of approaching traffic.

The child may function quite well in concrete areas and quite poorly in symbolic areas, yet many would have him spend hours in auditory training in which he is to discriminate high and low bell tones or to locate a ticking clock hidden in the classroom, when what he really needs are activities to help him use and understand the sounds and meanings of *words.*

Some children may receive the sensory messages strongly enough, but imperfectly: Some portion of the message may be distorted so that what he receives for later processing is in some way unlike the model he experienced. He may perceive as identical the letters *p* and *q,* or *b* and *d*—or may see *all* of these as the same. He may not perceive the roundness of a circle as different from the angular form of a pentagon. He may see the leaves clearly, but may not perceive that they are a part of the tree.

Faulty input of both symbolic and concrete areas is possible, too. The handicap these children face is far more obvious and far-reaching. The child whose problems in auditory perception include deficits in discriminating between sound/no sound, as well varying degrees of loudness, in locating the source of sound, and in interpreting loudness, may obviously have trouble in even arriving safely at school. Trying to make sense of what his teacher says in class is difficult enough; but, when he must be constantly alert to be sure whether or not she is speaking, his handicap is multiplied.

Differences in perception of symbolic and concrete tactile material may exist as well, and are of greatest interest to those working with the blind. We shall deal with the areas of touch, movement, and balance primarily as they function as areas which can be used to assist weaker visual or auditory areas.

Processing

Most teaching takes place in the input area. We present great masses of information in our best style often with extensive—and expensive—audio-visual aids, but it isn't until the child *processes* the information and makes it his own that learning takes place. This is the area where we have the least control.

As soon as material presented to the child in any modality acquires meaning—that is, as soon as perception takes place—processing begins. Rather than examine the neurological functioning at this point, we'll examine the educationally relevant events: First, image of whatever the child has seen, heard, felt, or done is stored as a memory, while he makes associations of that event with other occurrences of the same event, or similar events, or other sights, sounds, sensations, movements, or whatever other bits of information may be available. If sufficient related information is present and accessible, the child has "learned" something. If the information he received from his senses was faulty—either too weak or somehow distorted—then, no matter how well his brain is functioning, from then on, his conclusions may be in error.

As he evaluates and formulates ideas about new information presented by the senses, the child may change the modality of that information. When he reads aloud, he must change the visual symbols to sound symbols internally (and instantly) before he can pronounce the words. Likewise, when he hears the word *red*, he may change that auditory symbol to a visual color memory.

The bits of information stored as memory are stored in two ways: As simple memories, and with a sense of order. Some children have properly functioning memory systems, but very poorly functioning storage of a sense of order. Such a child may remember all the letters that make up a word, but not in the proper sequence. He may remember all the events which happened on the trip to the farm, but not which came first. Perhaps he recalls all the digits of his telephone number, but recalls them out of sequence.

The **processing** area is the most important area in terms of creative and cognitive functioning in the child, but this area cannot function well if defective functioning occurs in the input area. Input must occur in order for the child to have information to be processed; and the internal processing can use that information only as it is presented, whether perfect in detail, or distorted. The words the child pronounces, whether in imitation of the spoken word or from the printed representation, can be no better than the message that reached his brain.

With information of whatever quality, new problems can occur in the processing area, and can occur in a single modality, or can be more generalized. Some children may have adequate memory for things seen or touched, with poor recall of what has been heard. Such a child *seems* to ignore or daydream rather than to have a memory problem, because he *can* "remember every signpost between here and Memphis," but *can't* remember the three things he was *told* to do before he could go out to play. He is the child who elicits "If I've told you once, I've told you a thousand times!" from his exasperated parents.

Another child may have difficulty connecting the information he has previously learned in one modality, with material presented in a different modality. Told not to name, but to *describe* an object making a particular sound, the child may be unable to do so because he cannot "call up" a mental image of that object.

Output

The child's output is what the teacher examines to determine what he has learned. To find out what he has seen on the field trip, she has him tell or write about the experience. If his input and processing areas are intact, but his ability to write or put things into spoken language are defective, he may wrongly be judged as having gained little from the experience.

In many ways, the simplicity of the output area is devious and deceptive. It is easy to examine output: We simply have the child write, talk, **read** aloud, gesture, or perform some motor act. If his performance is poor, we say he has failed. Too rarely do we ask *where* in the process he has failed.

If we say to a child, "Jeff, go to the closet and bring me that big red book on the second shelf," and he returns a few seconds later with a puzzled look, what went wrong?

Maybe he just forgot what we said.

Maybe he remembered, but got things out of order. He remembered "second shelf" first, so he went to the toy shelf. There was no book.

Maybe he got distracted along the way, and "Busy Betty" brought us the book before he had a chance.

Maybe when he got there, there were so many books—reddish-brown, brownish-red, red-orange—that he wasn't sure which one it was. And how big is "big?"

Maybe he *does* remember what he hears, but that was too many things: Do what? Go where? Closet. On shelf (second), then do what? Bring who? Me? What? Book (big, red)?

An even simpler example of our frequently falling into the "trap of simplicity" in output is this math paper, as shown on the following page.

The teacher saw the wrong answers but not the error. She thought Jimmy failed simple computation. What Jimmy failed was "sign-noticing." He adds well. We have no information at all as to how well he performs in subtraction. Calling this a "math" failure makes as much sense as grading a child's physical education performance on "tennis-shoe-remembering" or "having-socks-marked-with-name" behavior!

Unfortunately, how the child processes and evaluates what he has perceived must be made at the output level. It is at this point that the child *does* something about the material to which he has been exposed: He says something, writes something, performs some action; or perhaps he engages in what is at this level of learning, a highly stylized form of talking: reading aloud.

Even if the earlier two processes, input and processing, are functioning properly, something can go wrong when the child tries to "do something" about what he has learned. The words he has chosen to say won't "come out," or part of the sentence he has formulated to write "slips away." The child may, at worst, be thought to be retarded because, although he has learned, his learning disability prevents him from demonstrating what he has learned. A more insightful observer may eventually perceive the real problem, but may, unfortunately, never go beyond labeling the child "expressive aphasic" or "dysgraphic."

```
50 E                    Jimmy

  2      6      9      8
 +3     +4     -1     +2
 ──     ──     ──     ──
  5     10     10 ✗   10


  6      8      6      9
 -4     -5     +5     -3
 ──     ──     ──     ──
 10 ✗   13 ✗   11     12 ✗
```

Ways of varying the output required are necessary if the real problem is to be determined. We say, "Katy can't make the y in her name. Katy must have a perceptual problem!" Perhaps we need to look again:

Can Katy match y's if we give her 3" x 5" cards with properly and improperly drawn y's?

Can Katy pick out the "right" *y* from a group of samples?

Can Katy *copy* a *y*?

If we show her a "proper" *y*, and then remove it, can Katy remember long enough to pick out another from samples, or to draw it?

We may discover that Katy can always spot the proper *y*, whether match-to-sample or from memory. That might hint that her perceptual processes were in good shape. Perhaps Katy's problem, on this sort of close inspection, turns out to be an output problem. Perhaps she makes the *y* backwards because she makes the wrong stroke first and, although she knows how she *wants* it to look, it "doesn't come out right."

Looking again, and looking several ways, can help us pinpoint problems which *are* output, and discriminate them from problems which occur earlier in the learning sequence.

While the specialist has many tests and special techniques for pinpointing areas of difficulty, the classroom teacher will usually have to depend on those old, often underrated standbys, classroom observation and common sense, to help her track down and deal with problems which prevent the child from learning normally.

This chapter has presented a sketchy theoretical framework for examining the "learning styles" of children. That basic idea is that even children of similar overall ability can vary widely in the learning style which will give them the greatest success.

The chapters which follow suggest a dichotomous view of children's learning: that some children learn best visually; others, auditorily. While we know that there are still many factors influencing learning ability, this dichotomous beginning allows the regular classroom teacher an opportunity to come closer to the goal of truly individualizing without intensive, technical labor for which her training may not have prepared her. It allows all children an opportunity to learn in the way which suits them best, and it will allow many children with slight learning problems to function *well* in regular classrooms.

For our purposes here, a "visual learner" is a child who learns best visually, whether (1) his visual learning channel is intact, but his auditory learning channel is defective, (2) his visual and auditory channels are both defective, but the visual channel is superior, or (3) his visual and auditory channels are both above average, but the visual channel is superior. An "auditory learner" is one who learns best auditorily, whether (1) his auditory channel is intact, but his visual learning channel is defective, (2) his auditory and visual channels are both defective, but the auditory channel is superior, or (3) his auditory and visual channels are both above average, but the auditory channel is superior.

The teacher checklists presented in this book are intended as a screening guide. You may want to use them to help you "zero in" on children's learning styles, and continue to use them until you can get through the waiting list for more extensive diagnostic services! They're not intended to replace those services, but only to provice an additional tool based on your own observations.

Those who are familiar with my book for learning-disabled children know that it contains similar checklists for the students themselves to respond to.[*] You may prefer to use those lists to get information on new students whom you don't know well enough to evaluate with the teacher's checklists. If you use both lists, you may find that you and the student may disagree on some items! If your informal reading tests clearly establish that the student's comprehension is better on oral reading, trust your judgment. If however, the student indicates he prefers riddles and verbal word games to crossword puzzles or checkers, perhaps you'd better take his word for it!

Not all items are on both lists. The student, for example, would have no way of knowing whether or not he "seems brighter than test scores indicate." Remember, these lists are not a fine diagnostic instrument—they are screening devices to give you a point from which to begin.

All teachers (and parents, too) will find that this simple way of looking at children's learning can improve the functioning of their students. The astute teacher will find that he or she is now able to look further and begin to deal creatively with even more complicated differences in learning.

---

[*]Marnell L. Hayes, *The Tuned-In, Turned-On Book about Learning Problems* (San Rafael, California: Academic Therapy Publications, 1974).

Chapter 3

The Auditory Learner

The child who exhibits a large number of the "classroom clues" described here should be referred for a thorough visual examination, not just a classroom screening. If he has a "clean bill of health" in terms of visual acuity, then the material in this section may help you help him.

1. His attention to visual tasks may be poor.

2. He seems bored or restless during silent filmstrips.

3. He attends more to the sound than to the screen during films shown in class.

4. His handwriting is poor.

5. His drawing or other artwork is poor, and he doesn't enjoy art activities.

6. Work he copies from the board may often turn out badly.

7. He may have reversals or inversions in writing, or he may leave out whole words or parts of words.

8. **He might prefer word games, riddles, and noisy or active toys and games to more visually oriented games like checkers, other board games, or jigsaw or crossword puzzles.**

9. He may rub his eyes or show other signs of eye problems, or complain that his eyes bother him.

10. He may do poorly on written spelling work, but he may be a better speller in spelling "bees."

11. He may not remember much of what he has read, and he does better on material discussed in class.

12. He may read below grade level, or below the level expected for his general ability.

13. His comprehension is probably better on oral reading than on silent reading.

14. His math errors, carefully analyzed, may show consistent patterns: inattention to signs, confusion of similar numerals, etc.

15. He may not seem to observe things other children comment on: new bulletin board displays, a broken window, or teacher's new dress.

16. He may do poorly on map activities.

17. He may do poorly on sight words and flashcard drills.

18. He may be poor at visual word attack so that he confuses words which look similar, such as *bill, bell, ball,* and *bull.*

19. He may do poorly on matching activities, especially where a series of lines must be drawn from one column to another.

20. He probably dislikes "ditto" activities, but given the chance, will sort through a stack of dittos for the clearest copy.

21. He may often skip words or even whole lines in reading, and uses his finger as a "pointer" whenever possible.

22. He may enjoy memory work.

23. He may be a "mumbler," muttering or whispering to himself during silent reading or other quiet seat work. He may also whistle or hum without being aware of it, rather than "doodling" on scratch paper.

24. He may have trouble identifying "how many?" without counting.

25. He seems brighter than his IQ test scores or achievement scores would lead you to believe—he "talks a good game."

26. His papers are probably poorly organized; often he writes the answer in the wrong blank on workbook pages, or can't find where the answers go.

27. He may seem lost on material requiring a separate answer sheet.

28. He has trouble locating words in the dictionary or index, and has trouble telling time.

29. Usually, his spelling errors "make sense" in that the child spells the word the way it sounds: *meen* for *mean*, etc.

30. He may have trouble numbering a paper in sequence.

The foregoing clues describe a child who shows discrepancy between his visual and auditory learning channels, with the auditory channel superior. When the visual channel is mildly deficient, as in the case of the child who exhibits only a few of these symptoms (perhaps less than one third of them), we may simply consider this a *learning difference*; when the visual channel shows marked discrepancy from the auditory, as in the child who exhibits many of these symptoms, the child may be diagnosed by experts as having a *visual learning disability*. For our purposes, it may be more appropriate to take a positive approach: consider the child's strengths, and refer to him as an *auditory learner*. this gives a direction to the efforts needed to help the child learn, particularly to the teacher's role in presenting new material. It especially helps keep firmly in mind the fact that the child is more *learner* than *disabled*; and that the teacher's role is to *teach*, rather than to cure.

Whether the auditory area is at, above, or below "average," the fact that it is superior to the visual area makes it the modality of choice for critical teaching and learning. The emphasis for this child is on hearing and speaking. His best sources are your voice, his own voice, and tapes and records. He needs to learn to change visual material to auditory-verbal material whenever possible. He needs encouragement to listen, and assurance that his auditory skills are a source of strength.

Here are some specific, subject matter related suggestions:

Reading

Phonics-based approaches are the methods of choice for this child. Visual methods using extensive initial sight word vocabularies will result in **frustration**. The child needs to learn phonics word attack skills, and needs to be taught to read aloud as much as possible. Unfamiliar words can be "sounded out" far more successfully aloud; and the child can, by "filling in the blanks," make more successful attempts at difficult words which may tend not to follow phonics rules.

As soon as possible, the child should be taught to re-auditorize without vocalizing aloud. This can have the same effect as vocalizing aloud, and becomes a study skill that the child can use even in adulthood, although occasional vocalizing aloud for difficult or critical material will still be helpful. Young children can learn to re-auditorize silently when told to "say it out loud inside your head." Often, having the child close his eyes and "listen" to the word, blending the sounds aloud or silently, is helpful.

For older children, making tapes of their reading for playback, or reading aloud with another child or with the teacher, may provide auditory review. Serving as a tutor for a younger child or slower reader can be useful in practice and an enormous self-concept booster.

Writing

The child with visual learning problems who leaves out words or phrases, has trouble copying, or who seems to have trouble writing words he knows well, can be taught to "talk to himself" while writing. When he reads the word or sentence from the board, he should repeat it to himself over and over as he transfers it to his paper. He can begin by talking aloud; later, he can re-auditorize silently.

The younger child who is just learning to write can "talk" the letters as he learns to write them. At first, the teacher may want to assist, giving the cues aloud to the child: "We're going to write the capital letter A. Remember A? It goes down, down, and across-in-the-middle. Capital E goes down, and the front has out, out, out." It is best to repeat the cue first; then repeat while making the letter; and finally, have the child repeat with you while he makes the letter. It may be helpful in cases of severe visual problems, especially perceptual problems, to have the child "talk" the letter several times, then "write" it with a fingertip while "talking" it before using pencil, to prevent the distorted vision from interfering with the auditory learning. The child with visual problems frequently has trouble remembering which strokes come first, and the "chants" he uses for the letters will serve as reminders of both formation and order. Tracing exercises, using tracing paper and pencil, or acetate sheets and transparency marker to trace letters or words *under supervision* (to prevent practicing an error) while "talking" the letters or words, is a good way to set the auditory and visual motor patterns in tune.

Spontaneous writing of older children can be improved by having the child formulate his sentences aloud; then by having him repeat them as often as necessary as he writes them. This is useful for copying from the board, too. Tell the child to read the material, a sentence at a time, and repeat it once or twice. He then should write it, seeing how many words he can remember before he has to look back at the board. The child can learn to use this technique for short answer questions as well as lengthy essays. High-school, college-age, or adult auditory learners may work far better composing with a dictating machine or at the typewriter than with pen or pencil.

Arithmetic

Counting, set recognition, and learning math combinations need auditory cues for learning. Visual set recognition may be very poor, but the child can learn to count aloud or silently in order to group. Math combinations, most frequently taught visually, need special adjustment. Just repeating the combinations as well as the solutions, aloud, or chanting or singing them, with a visual check for correctness, may be the simplest method. Tapes, teacher-made or made by the child himself, may be useful. Speed of sight recognition with flash cards may be slow, as the child initially will at least need to repeat the entire combination sequence, not just the answer. Often, it is helpful for the child to follow this sequence: "Look at the problem, and repeat it aloud. Close your eyes and repeat it again, filling in the answer. Look at the answer side of the card, and repeat it again. If you were wrong, repeat the correct answer one or more times."

More complex work, such as "story problems," benefits from vocalization. Have the child read the problem aloud, and plan aloud his "strategy" to reach the solution.

Spelling

The auditory learner is not a good candidate for the "write-the-words-five-times-each" school of spelling practice. He needs to look at the words—using his finger as a pointer to help prevent visual error—and spell them. Having the words "called out" by a buddy or parent is a good technique. The traditional spelling bee format, "table, t-a-b-l-e, table" is especially appropriate for this child. At test time, the child should listen to the word as the teacher pronounces it, pronounce and spell it to himself, and write it as he silently says each letter. Remind the child with serious visual problems to close his eyes if necessary during study or test sequences, in order to block out distracting or inaccurate visual images.

Other Academic Areas

For young children, the teacher should present new material with as much auditory stimulation as possible. Class discussion, teacher talk, tapes, and records are helpful. The older child who must read in an academic area, such as social studies, should read aloud or re-auditorize. Poor readers should have access to taped material. Having the child "read along" with the tape can provide additional reading practice. The very poor reader may do better if he listens only, with his eyes closed. Having the material read aloud to the child, perhaps by an older child who needs practice reading somewhat below his independent reading level, is also effective.

In any area where the child must learn primarily visual material, such as map work, identifying the parts of a microscope, or learning football plays from charts, the child needs to be taught to transfer the material to his auditory-verbal channel. The child can look at the material—using a finger or other pointer to keep his place—and read, discuss, or describe as necessary:

"OK, this is a map of Texas. That border up there by Oklahoma is the Red River. Down at the bottom is the Rio Grande . . . ." Or, "Well, that's the *stage* of the microscope, and up here is the *ocular*, spelled o-c-u-l-a-r . . . ." If the child must memorize lists (and it's astonishing how many teachers want children to memorize the names of the Kings of England, or the names of manned space ships), he can learn them just as he learned the alphabet from the "Alphabet Song" or the months of the year from another useful ditty. He can invent tunes or rhymes. The teacher (perhaps the resource teacher helping the child with "**mainstream**" homework, for surely no special educator would assign such lists!) can help the child devise acronyms as mnemonic devices. These nonsense words cue the child to the order of the list, as they are formed by the first letter of each word in sequence—as a special aid. I myself once helped a college friend learn to spell her boy friend's twelve-letter "ethnic" surname by turning it into a rah-rah cheer!

Examine classroom routines carefully. Evaluate your procedures, and see which ones might well be changed to fit the auditory learner's style. Do you use individual work folders for your students, with a cover sheet listing each assignment for the day? Consider using a pocket-type folder with a tape cassette for assignments. (It might speed your cassette preparation time, too, if *written* assignments are not necessary for each child.) You may "go creative" and tape interesting sounds or messages in between assignments, something like this:

"This is your first assignment. Please get this week's spelling list and call the words out to Nancy. When you are finished, come back for a special message. Turn off the recorder when you hear the tone. BEEP!" When the child completes the assignment, he turns on the recorder for the short song or joke, followed by his next assignment.

Your good auditory learner's self-concept may gain if you use his ability, and give him occasional (or frequent) tutorial duties, assisting the child who has auditory problems. The students can trade about, with the auditory learner receiving help and supervision from visual learners on visual remedial work. The teacher cannot supervise eight to thirty students simultaneously and individually, so that all too often, a child "practices his error." Teaming children for some work periods can work wonders. Often, too, your student tutors will come up with new ideas and suggestions which can help more than the finest professional materials.

The child with auditory learning ability above and beyond his visual ability needs to see his auditory skills as an asset which can be of constant use. Emphasis on his auditory *ability* rather than his visual *disability* is self-concept building, too. Letting the child "show off" when his skills can come into play is also a good technique: "That was a long list of things we needed for our picnic. Jimmy is so good at remembering what he hears—maybe he can call the items out to me while I write them on the board." Dramatic work, producing taped materials of "sound effects" for those who need auditory remediation, carrying verbal messages—any vehicle which allows the child to see himself in a positive light and to learn the value of this stronger learning channel, should be utilized.

Special Materials for the Auditory Learner

The suggestions above make it clear that the teacher's voice and the child's own voice may be the best tools for the auditory learner. Beyond these, an extremely helpful tool is the tape recorder: any kind, size, or price. This device, once so expensive that few classrooms had them, can now be had so cheaply that they are within the range of nearly every budget. Also useful, but less flexible because it uses only commercially prepared lessons, is the record player. Making tape recordings need not be a major portion of the teacher's time. As the suggestions above have indicated, a child can often make his own tapes. A teacher aide or another student can help Tapes can be re-used, or used for more than one student. Tape recorders equipped with headphones are especially helpful, as they can be used by one child without disturbing the rest of the class.

Many other commercial materials are available, with new ones appearing on the market constantly. Investigate new items carefully, but keep in mind that if either of two materials will produce a given result, the simplest, least complicated, and most obvious one is usually the best. When in doubt, ask the child's opinion. Although he may not be able to verbalize all his reactions, his preferences and opinions may very well be based on his **needs**. The same sort of response that leads the child with poor visual skills automatically to use his index finger to keep his place in reading, will help him make choices appropriate for him in **other** areas.

Chapter 4

The Visual Learner

No simple symptom is sufficient evidence of an auditory learning problem; however, when a child exhibits several of the following "classroom clues," it's time to take a closer look. A hearing test is a must!

1. He may seem to ignore verbal directions.

2. Questions or instructions must often be repeated, frequently in different words.

3. He may frequently have a "blank" expression on his face, or may seem to daydream during classes which are primarily verbal.

4. He may substitute gestures for words, or may seem, by his gestures, to be literally groping for a word.

5. He may have poor speech, in terms of either low vocabulary, poor flexibility of vocal patterns, or articulation.

6. He may watch the teacher's lips closely, and may be distressed when he cannot see her face, such as when she is talking while writing on the blackboard, or discussing a filmstrip in a darkened room.

7. He often looks to see what everyone else is doing before following instructions.

8. He may play the TV, tape, or record player too loudly.

9. He may say "What?" or "Huh?" often.

10. He seems to misunderstand often.

11. He often speaks too loudly, though he may dislike speaking before the group or listening to others.

12. He prefers the "Show" aspects of "Show and Tell," and prefers filmstrips to tapes.

13. He may have trouble discriminating similar words or sounds that he hears: *Bill, bell, bull,* and *ball* may all sound the same to him, and he certainly cannot discriminate *pin* from *pen.*

14. He may do poorly in phonics-based activities.

15. He often can't remember information given verbally.

16. He may describe things in terms of visual stimuli, and omit auditory descriptive material.

17. He prefers visual games, such as board games, or active games and toys, to those which involve listening or speaking.

18. His speech may be inappropriate for his age; or he may not have learned the language patterns of his home (even if the home patterns are not Standard American English).

19. He may have trouble associating sounds and objects.

20. He may substitute words similar in sound or meaning for one another.

21. He seems to know few words' synonyms commonly known by children at his age or ability level.

22. He may "get lost" in rote verbalizations, even the alphabet, rote counting, or memorizing his times tables.

23. He may not enjoy music as much as he enjoys art work.

24. He may have a speech defect; if so, it is probably an articulation problem.

25. He may respond less rapidly than his peers to unusual sounds: a far-off siren; a record player or musical instrument in a nearby classroom.

26. He may do better work when he is to do what is demonstrated, not told to him verbally.

27. He doesn't seem as bright as his test scores indicate.

28. He may be unable to explain in words many complex tasks he is able to do, such as repairing his bicycle, taking apart a clock, etc.

29. He often answers with a simple *yes* or *no*, rarely using complex sentences.

30. He can look up a word in a dictionary fairly quickly if he has the spelling, though he may have to recite half the alphabet to find the right sections; but he's completely lost if he must look it up in order to determine the spelling.

The child whose hearing is normal, but who exhibits a number of the characteristics just listed, could be described as having *auditory-verbal learning problems*. Referral for a thorough evaluation by a learning disabilities specialist may provide valuable insight and information into the specific nature of the problem, as well as to appropriate remedial tactics. With the teacher's observations based on these characteristics, we can consider the child in a more positive light, and classify him as a *visual learner*. Whether his auditory-verbal difficulties are mild, suggesting learning difference, or severe, indicating the presence of a learning disability, we can use visual approaches to maximize his educational gains.

This child's eyes are his keys to learning. He needs to look at what he is to learn; to have materials kept in front of him; to be alert to the visual world. He needs help in learning to revisualize what he has seen, and to change what he *hears* into visual images for learning.

The child with auditory learning problems may ask often for repetition of instructions. This usually means that the child has not understood rather than that he did not hear, but first try repeating the same instructions, adding additional information. If the problem is simply that he did not *hear* (as possible for the learning-disabled child as for you and me) he can respond and "save face." If the child still doesn't understand, then rephrase. For example: you say, "Johnny, bring me your workbook." He says "Huh?" thinking, "Look? Book? Cook?" You say, "Bring me your workbook—the workbook for math." If he *still* misunderstands, you say, "We need to work on math. Get your red *Fun With Math* workbook.

Reading

Look-and-say and experience chart approaches are ideal for the visual learner. Phonics skills need to be shelved until the child has a strong sight-word vocabulary, then, the phonics skills should be introduced gradually with reference to parallel sight words: "That word looks like the other word you know, except for the first letter. Look at the word you know—*ball*. Now look at the new word [*tall*]. They rhyme—what could it be?"

Reading instruction for this child should always be held near a chalkboard, chart stand, or with notepad and marker handy to present visual cues as necessary. The child needs to learn to call up visual images of similar words for comparison in word attack, and needs to learn to use context clues to help him work out words which don't follow the same rules as any of his sight words. New words can be printed on cards with bright marking pens for visual review. (Unless the child is visually distractible, recycle used computer cards into excellent cheap, disposable flash cards).

Any of the commercial reading approaches based on visual methods can be used with this child. The child can be encouraged to close his eyes and "look" at his mental image of the story again in order to answer comprehension questions. Having the child glance briefly over the text material or flash cards before written exercises or tests, can be helpful.

Writing

The visual learner grasps the differences between letters easily, and learns to write with little difficulty. Attempts at writing new words which the child has heard but not seen may result in failure, or in the child's writing a visually similar word. To transfer material from one location to another, such as from chalkboard to paper, the child can learn to look at the material, and then write it, "looking at the picture of it" in his mind.

Visual learning children who can recognize and form the letters, but who have trouble remembering the *sounds* of the letters, can benefit from having a set of letter cards with "sound pictures" for each. These can be simple line drawings of objects with the letter sound strongly featured in the most common name for the object. Have the child help select the picture for each card. When the child faces the letter in a word not in his sight vocabulary, the visual memory of the "sound picture" can help cue him to the new word.

In writing from dictation, as in taking notes or writing assignments, the child should be told to visualize the words, and write them from that image rather than from what he has heard. Similarly, the older child, whose essay writing suffers from direct transfer of his auditory problem of poorly formulated sentences, can learn to "imagine" the words in print, rearranging them mentally. Letting the child be free to mark over or write in as much as necessary until he has his rough draft in good form, can help the visual learner greatly.

For the older child in a regular classroom, the teacher's help with class notes can be invaluable. The teacher should correct the child's spelling, *not by marking words wrong* for the child to correct, but by rewriting the words correctly. Words written incorrectly are often then learned incorrectly from the strong visual image the child has produced. Having the child make notes in pencil, so that errors can be erased and rewritten correctly by the teacher, is a good plan. This should be done nonpunitively, so that the child understands that he is being helped by being provided good visual clues. This is often helpful to the older visual-learner whose note-taking is slow because he fears making errors in his notes.

Arithmetic

Visual aids, such as flash cards, concrete items, and set cards, are most useful with this child. The child needs to look at materials, and often to touch them, in counting. The child's ability to recognize groups can help him in weak areas such as rote counting. Flash cards for math combinations are a must. For very young children, cards with numerals and a matching set of pictures or dots help provide a visual picture of the meaning of the numerals.

The visual learner is often a "whiz" at simple math computation, but poor at written problems which are not set up for him. With these "story problems," the child may need to visualize the problem, imagining the objects or details, and manipulating them mentally or by drawing them on paper as he seeks the solution.

As early as possible, the child should be taught to use his fingers as computational devices. Too many children are prevented from using these useful tools, and they spend a great amount of time drawing groups of sticks in the margins of their math papers when they could learn to use "calculators" which are always with them: their fingers. Many adults with IQ's in the superior range count on their fingers for speed and accuracy. Some teachers consider counting on the fingers a "bad math habit." A little thought should convince any thinking person that it is preferable to have a child with a bad math habit than a child with no math skills.

Some additional math computational aids useful for the visual learner are discussed in the chapter on tactile-kinesthetic aids, but here is a visual boost for multiplication useful for children who continue to want to use the "sticks drawn in the margin" method.

For example, to multiply 5 x 3, instead of drawing five sets of three sticks and counting them, show the child how to draw five lines one way

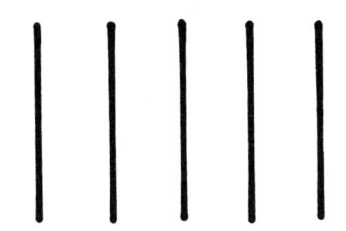

|||||

and "cross" (X) them with three lines:

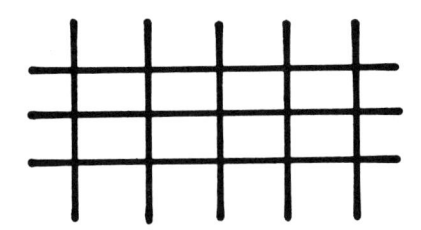

Then he counts the *intersections:*

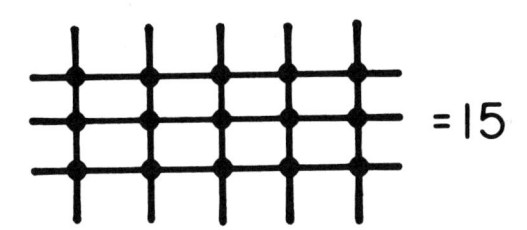

= 15

This is especially useful for showing multiplication by 0. For example, 3 x 0 would be done thus: Three lines

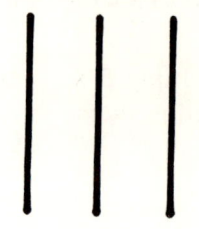

| | |

with no lines crossing them. The child has *no* intersections to count, so that he can easily see that his answer is 0.

Spelling

The visual learner is often poor in spelling "bees," but may function well in written spelling work. His study needs to be visual, rather than the "have Mother call them out to you" variety. Writing the words several times each is good, *as long as the words are written correctly the first time,* and as long as the child does not see this as a punitive measure. (Children who have had multiple-writing tasks assigned as punishment do not benefit much from this approach without a good bit of insightful counseling.) Tracing with transparency pen, or even tracing multiple-copied spelling lists with felt-tipped pens can be helpful in linking the visual image with the proper motor pattern.

The child should learn to write new words, whether spelling words on tests, or words to be used in other written work, by "looking at the picture of the word in his mind, and then copying it from the picture." This can help the child through what is, for him, especially difficult: oral spelling, where in he must hear the word and process it properly before he can write it. One Mississippi eight-year-old, taught to visualize spelling words before writing them, brought his spelling grades from failing to near-consistent 100's. He still occasionally forgot, usually on the sentence **dictation** his teacher included at the end of each test. One error he made was when the teacher dictated a sentence beginning with the word *our*. Doug wrote it just as his southern teacher pronounced it: "*Awer.*" Asked later, he could indeed spell *our*: "I just forgot to look at the picture in my head."

Home study, with the words called out by a parent or sibling, can be valuable if the child is encouraged to write the words, then spell them back for checking. The child should use pencil, skip lines, and erase and rewrite misspelled words.

Other Academic Areas

For visual learning children, the teacher should present new material with as much visual stimulation as possible. Pictures, drawings, films, slides, filmstrips, and the written word, depending on the age of the child, are helpful. *All* assignments should be written on the board or on an assignment sheet. (The visual learner needs to learn early to carry a small pocket calendar. I myself, a strong visual learner and profoundly poor auditory one, go into shock when my appointment book is mislaid even for a few moments!)

Individual instructions should be done with chalkboard or paper close at hand. Illustrate what you're saying. Often, a line drawing, or a few written words, will serve to cue a child to the overall context. Be sure, though, that you don't write while talking. The visual learner needs to "see" the words as you speak them. This means you'll need to sit opposite, not beside, the child for individual work. It helps if you are adept at reading, writing, and drawing upside down!

Keep visual stimuli at the child's level. New teachers (and, unfortunately, even some experienced ones) tend to write high on chalkboards, even for small groups or when a child is to come to the board to mark a word or work a problem. Try looking at it from a child's-eye level. Even if the child can reach the work, does the angle of vision distort it badly?

Whenever possible, keep visual clues before the child. For older children, a brief outline of material to be covered orally may be all that is necessary, even in a group. You can refer to it as appropriate: "That's Roman numeral II on your guide, Gary."

When textbooks are in short supply, the visual learner, who often reads well, needs a book as badly as the poor reader. Although he may actually be able to read the material during class time, he will need a textbook or good notes to help him recall material *discussed* in class. (His notes are often poor, as it takes so much concentration and time to transfer material from listening to writing, especially if distorted input must be sorted out *en route*.)

In any area where the child must learn auditory material, the child should be helped to revisualize wherever possible. For older children, outlining, underlining, or using "highlighting" marking pens, and taking notes from the text are good study approaches. Unfortunately, the child rarely has the opportunity to use books which can be marked or underlined.

The child in regular classes with teachers who do not understand his problem can be guided in devising his own study techniques. One enterprising seventh-grade girl reviewed some class discussion material about the state of Texas by spending two and a half hours one evening producing four maps, traced from the text and then painstakingly filled in according to areas discussed in the class and in the text: One of the major rivers, one of the Indian tribes, one of the geographic areas, and one of the geologic features. She summed up each in a brief paragraph. She learned more than a week's class discussion had taught her, and "convinced" the teacher to give her extra credit as well.

The visual learner can learn to make his own flash cards early in school. He can learn to deal with "oral teachers" by asking "Would you write that on the board for me?" rather than "How do you spell that?" New words should be written out, either in pencil, or just for tactile-kinesthetic cues to revisualization, on a desk top or other surface. An eleven-year-old gifted visual learner with fairly serious auditory problems asked her mother for words to describe the visual characteristics of tropical-fruit roll candies she was eating on a trip. She knew *transparent*, but wanted words for two other visual characteristics. From her definition, it was clear that the words she wanted were *translucent* and *opaque*. She asked how they were spelled, and, lacking paper to write them down, "wrote" them with a fingertip on her leg. Two weeks later, with no review, she remembered the words themselves, their definitions, and spelling. This same child keeps dozens of fine-tipped marking pens in rainbow colors for her own notes and study aids, and has learned to deal fairly well with a very serious auditory deficit. She is aware of her learning strengths, so that she can use them. Her parents are aware of her strengths and weaknesses, too. Although they may forget occasionally and start the old song that the child with auditory problems is so weary of, "If I've told you once . . . ," they also recognize and appreciate her strong learning pattern: She's the one who first sees the turn-off signs on automobile trips, and the first to spot the dropped water ski on trips to the lake for the family's favorite sport.

Review your classroom procedures for ways to add visual aids. Keep in mind that your own gestures and facial expressions are cues the visual learner has been using, consciously or not, for some time. Continue to let the child use these cues. Don't get so involved with other visual aids that the child can no longer use the only cues he'll be *sure* to find in other situations.

Special Materials for the Visual Learner

Anything "see-able" goes. The child needs things, pictures, and books. Filmstrips and movies are excellent, especially for the child who is reading below his general educational level.

Individual supplies useful for the visual learner include notecards, colored markers, crayons, paints, and gummed papers. Colored plastic paper clips mark pages without tearing them, and can be used to color-code for specific topics. Acetate sheets and transparency markers or grease pencils are valuable for tracing words to spell, maps, or math combinations. Pressure-stick labels which can be removed without tearing or leaving gummy spots are extremely useful for reminders on the refrigerator, on the front of a notebook, inside locker doors, on bedroom doors, or on desk tops. They come in a variety of sizes and shapes. Clipboards to hold notes or tracing papers prevent materials from slipping. A bulletin board by the door at school is a good reminder for teachers and pupils alike, and another in the child's room at home is excellent. At home, magnet-held, taped, or pressure-stick notes, messages, reminders, and words of praise on the refrigerator or kitchen door are critical! Some families keep sets of children's magnet-held plastic letters for messages for one another. Many preschoolers "learn their letters" this way. The visual learner needs, and hence must carry, more books, papers, and supplies, so a backpack (fashionable) or a school bag (practical) but apparently not "in" if the child is over eight years of age!) is essential.

If the visual learner is also visually distractible, the attractive "gear" needed for good visual learning needs to be stored well out of sight with individual items taken out only as needed; and a weekly desk clean-up is a must.

The visual learner needs to use plenty of paper—paper for notes, outlining, sketches, rough drafts, reminders and for just plain "doodling." Much of the paper he uses may seem to be "wasted"; but how much better to waste paper than to waste human brain power! The teacher who insists on crowding much into small spaces, or having children use both sides of every sheet of paper, runs the risk of creating more problems than are cured. Most learning disabilities teachers have seen more than one child who can write the first few of a list of words on a sheet of paper in standard left-to-right, no-reversal form; asked to continue on the back of the paper, the child sees the show-through from the front, and proceeds right-to-left, all letters reversed! (To avoid the distractions of show-through on child-produced, teacher-made, or commercial materials, slip a piece of black construction paper behind the page.)

While excellent remedial materials for visual problems have been on the market for several years, only recently has much appeared for the child with auditory learning problems. Remember to keep in mind that whenever possible, you should use the simplest materials, and those least likely to produce dependence. Use the materials only for children who need them, unless you can justify their use for an entire class on the basis of general enjoyment, or success experience for the auditory learner. Keep in mind that your goal in using the material is to improve the auditory functioning of the visual-learning child. If group usage will result in the auditory learner's shining *at the expense* of the visual learner, then you need to use the material individually, or for small groups divided according to learning modality.

Chapter 5

Touch-and-Do Learning

For the child with deficits in both visual and auditory learning, the use of tactile-kinesthetic ("touch-and-do") cues is critical. For any other child, whether functioning normally in both channels with only slight differences, or defective in one channel, tactile-kinesthetic skills can give an extra boost to learning.

Tactile materials are intended to strengthen messages to the child's brain through the stimulation provided by textured surfaces. Kinesthetic cures involve the tension and relaxation of the muscles as they enable a limb to move in an action. In almost any material using tactile cues, kinesthetic factors operate, too, as the child is normally instructed to use the material by tracing over or around the surfaces with a finger tip. The texture and the tensions of the muscles as the child traces the form provide a memory pattern of how the shape is formed, thus assisting the child in re-creating the form later, or in identifying it when he sees it.

Perhaps the most commonly used tactile-kinesthetic materials are sandpaper letters. These tactile aids have become almost synonymous with "materials for learning-disabled children." Unfortunately, some teachers who use them do not realize that the benefit, as is the case with any material, is in its proper use, not in material itself. Much teacher time has been spent cutting sandpaper letters, ruining many pairs of scissors and giving teachers gooseflesh from the very characteristics of the tactile stimulation they seek to utilize! Much money has been spent on the purchase of commercially-prepared sandpaper letters. For the time and money invested in this material to bear fruit, a better understanding of the function of the tactile letters is in order.

Generally, the child takes the letter card, and traces over the letter with his fingertip. Properly prepared, the card is as error-proof as possible. That is, the child should easily get the right side up; and, as long as his finger is on the rough surface, the form of that surface should prevent his making strokes not needed to form that letter.

These are the two areas where many teacher-made and commercial sandpaper letters fail. First, the usual method of getting the right side up (if this is done at all!) is for the material to be used only under teacher supervision. Some letter sets do have a slashed corner, as computer cards do, indicating the top right-hand or left-hand corner. Considering the amount of time which must often be spent teaching learning-disabled children left/right, top/bottom, one can easily see the weakness in this method. Drawing a familiar picture at the bottom of the card is *better*, but may be a distraction in and of itself. The author cuts a notch at the center bottom of each card:

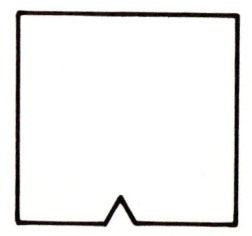

The child can quickly learn always to turn the card so that the "teepee" or "Indian house" sits on the desk surface.

The second error-proofing failure is in the form of the letters. Consider what happens when the child is to learn the capital A, which has three "points":

but the letter he is to trace with his finger is a block A, with six "points":

If he traces this letter, he may think that eleven pencil strokes are necessary to form the letter A! After all, that's how many straight edges his exploring finger tip will find. Obviously, he is intended to trace down the center of the "legs" and crossbar of the letter. If he is able to do this, then his visual perception is such that he probably does not need the tactile-kinesthetic boost at all! Why not simply mark the letter with bright marking pen on a square of

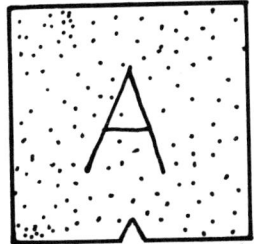

sandpaper? Why the time and expense involved in two layers of material, separately cut and then glued together?

When these two failure possibilities are examined, it becomes easy to see that the "lazy way" of making tactile letters may be the best: Write the letter with a *thin* line of white glue, and sprinkle with sand. For a deluxe touch, glitter or plastic reflective beading (the kind used on greeting cards and highway signs) can be substituted, but it adds to the expense and is functionally no better.

Not only can the teacher produce the material more rapidly and cheaply this way, there is also an added advantage in that the material is welcomed even by children who found the real sandpaper letters as "creepy" as fingernails scratching a chalkboard!

Another frequently used material in many learning disability classrooms is the "feelie bag" or "feelie box." The child is expected to reach into a box and discriminate by touch between, say, a swatch of burlap and one of velvet. From a purely practical standpoint, there is little educational relevance of this task, unless the child's ability to learn is seriously defective in all channels. Too often, we borrow activities or remedial techniques because they are clever or "cute," but without examining our objectives or the stated objectives of the developer of that material. As a tool for exploring the senses in early childhood programs, or as one of many remedial devices for children with learning deficits in all areas, the "feelie box" has value. It is not so generally useful as its frequent presence in classrooms might suggest.

Other materials which can provide tactile and/or kinesthetic cues for learning include the salt or meal tray, or the clay pan.

For the salt or meal tray, any granular substance is placed in a thin layer in a tray, box lid, or shallow pan. The child "writes" with a fingertip, with the pushing aside of the granules providing tactile and kinesthetic stimulation. The clay pan uses ordinary plastic-type modeling clay rolled flat in a pan. The child uses a stylus or plain pencil for writing, with the drag of the thick clay providing increased kinesthetic awareness. A college-age girl with written communication problems so serious that "dysgraphia" seemed an appropriate term, found that a grease pencil or chinamarking pencil provided sufficient "drag" both to slow her writing so that all the words "made it" from brain to paper, and to increase the strength of now-correct writing patterns.

Using a single sheet of newsprint over ordinary window screening or nylon net, and writing with crayon or pencil, provides good tactile-kinesthetic practice, even for older children who are working on spelling, math combinations, or similar tasks. "Writing" on the screen (or a rough canvas notebook cover) with a blunt stylus or even a finger tip, can provide this kind of practice without the use of paper. A newsprint pattern can be placed under the screen, and the tracing can be done with large strokes with a stylus, retractable ball-point pen with the point retracted, or eraser end of a pencil.

The child may want to provide more massive kinesthetic clues for himself. He may enjoy "walking" out his spelling words or "riding" them with his bicycle. The child may even enjoy "writing" his work with a penlight in a dark room, using a blank wall as a screen.

Another aid some children find useful is tapping out rhythms of words, either by letters or syllables, or adding finger tapping to counting on fingers as a math aid. Many children develop the "math tapping" on their own; some, as a way to count on their fingers under the desk where the teacher can not see to stop them. Teachers sometimes observe the child who must tap in a certain way—perhaps on the end of his nose!

The kinds of tactile-kinesthetic cues useful vary widely from one individual to another. Some benefit most form smaller materials, such as the clay tray or sandpaper letters, which can be used at a desk. Others find rhythms and tapping most useful. Still others find the whole-body involvement best. Try some of the following, keeping in mind that what's best for one won't necessarily be best for all.

1. Make tactile letters or words:

Make sand or glitter letter- or word-cards as described above.

For children who have progressed to cursive writing, forming the words in yarn or string on a pattern card, then glueing it down, may be helpful. Both forming the word, and using it for tracing when dry, provide useful cues. Be sure that the word is properly formed—this is, with loops and retracings exactly as it would be written, not cut and pieced together.

Some children, especially older boys, respond better to "wiring" the words. Use any flexible wire. Cloth-covered electrical wire is expensive, but it is colorful and can be re-used many times. The words can be "built" on the desk top, or stapled on paper or cardboard.

2. Provide an oversized number line somewhere in the classroom so that children can "walk out" their math problems. (Small number lines should *not* be glued on desk top for distractible or stimulus-bound children!)

3. Keep sufficient counters of various kinds on hand for math work—spools, buttons, plastic spoons, etc., and paper cups, margarine tubs, or cans to count them into. Remember to encourage changeover to counting on fingers as soon as possible, and changeover to memory as soon as possible after that.

4. Two finger-counting aids for math which have been found to be especially good for older children are multiplication methods. The first works only for the 9's tables and is useful only for children with no left-right discrimination problems. Let's say the problem is 3 x 9. Count on your fingers like this:

and turn down the finger with the number you wish to multiply by 9:

Now count the fingers which are left: On the left of the turned-down finger there are 2; on the right, there are 7. The answer is 2-7, or 27.

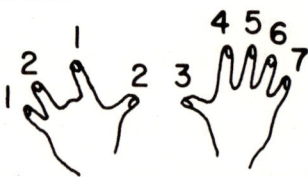

The second method works even for children with left-right confusion, and works for all combinations from 6 x 6 to 9 x 9.

It is described in *The Tuned-In, Turned-On Book About Learning Problems*. The child must already know the combinations lower than this. Most children have relatively little trouble learning the lower combinations; for those who haven't mastered them, this method is obviously inappropriate. The method seems complicated, and upon first exposure, seems more complex than memorizing the tables could *ever* be. However, the author has used this method even with intermediate retarded students with great success. The method seems to work with children because no matter how many steps must be gone through, each is concrete. Sheer memorization has no such built-in checking device.

Many teachers introduce the method by telling the child or group that they're about to learn a sure-fire "cheat-chart" that no teacher can take away from them! While some may question the ethics of this approach, they cannot doubt its attention-getting characteristics!

Here's how it works; but you can't learn it unless you put the book down and actually go through the steps:

First, remember that thumbs are sixes. Hold up both thumbs.

We'll do 7 x 8. Start with either hand, and count up from six for the first number; then on the other hand for the second number:

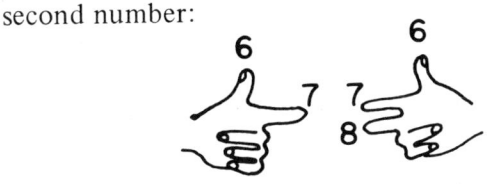

Now count all the "sticking-out" fingers by tens: 10-20-30-40-50.

Now multiply the "turned-down" fingers by each other: 3 x 2 = 6

$$50 + 6 = 56!$$

Try one more to be sure you've got it. We'll do 9 x 8. Count up from six, multiplier on one hand and multiplicand on the other:

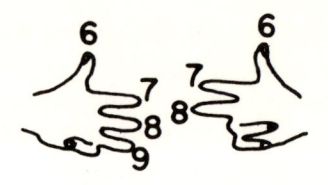

Count by tens: 10-20-30-40-50-60-70. Multiply the "turned-down" ones by each other: 1 x 2 = 2;

70 + 2 = 72.

This method can be made useful for children who learn best in any modality for there is the *visual* stimulus of the hands and **fingers**; the *auditory* stimulus which can be provided by counting aloud; and the *tactile-kinesthetic* stimulus of sticking out or turning down the fingers, or tapping them for counting. It can be used to study the tables or to check for accuracy.

Some teachers fear that this method will become a "crutch." One need only observe a child progress from using this method constantly, to occasionally, to the point where he starts sticking out fingers, glances at them, and "remembers" the answer without "counting up," to realize that the child will drop the crutch himself as soon as he sees that he can do the task more quickly without it.

There is a variation of this method which has the fingers touching at the points of the multiplier and multiplicand rather than some stuck out and some turned down, but this requires the child to remember whether he counts tens for the fingers above, below, and/or including the touching fingers. Using some fingers straight and some turned down is less confusing, especially for children who do not yet consistently manage above/below dichotomies.

The observant teacher may pick up many new clues to help just by watching. Frequently a child will quite unconsciously use some sort of tapping or other rhythmic behavior when he is concentrating on a new task. This can be a sign that this child is attuned to this type of learning aid and may benefit from more direct suggestions as to how to use this system.

Mnemonic devices can help children with those rote memorization tasks so many teachers still insist on. How many teachers recall being in elementary school, and thinking that *arithmetic* and *geography* were surely the longest, hardest words we'd ever have to spell! Then someone suggested that they were easy to spell if we'd just remember two silly sentences: For *arithmetic*, "*A R*ed *I*ndian *T*hought *H*e *M*ight *E*at *T*urnips *I*n *C*hurch!" For *geography*, "*G*eorge *E*liot's *O*ld *G*randfather *R*an *A P*ig *H*ome *Y*esterday!"

Later, in high school, perhaps you learned Linnaeus' classification system in this way: "*K*ing *P*hillip *C*ame *O*ver *F*rom *G*reece to *S*pain," for Kingdom, Phylum, Class, Order, Family, Genus, Species. Or Moh's Scale of hardness: "*T*all *G*irls *C*an *F*lirt *A*nd *M*any *Q*ueer *T*hings *C*an *D*o"—that's Talc, Typsum, Calcite, Flourite, Apatite, Microline, Quartz, Topaz, Corundum, Diamond. You may know many, many others. You can help your students devise such devices for especially difficult things they want to learn. Combined with hand-clapping or other rhythmic behavior, many children have learned to spell

"M - I - crookedletter - crookedletter - I -
crookedletter - crookedletter - I -
longtail - longtail - I!"

Perhaps the areas of "touch-and-do" learning is the one wherein the teacher's creativity has the greatest chance to shine.

Chapter 6

Interference: A Special Set Of Problems

These interference problems are simply that: behaviors or reactions which can interfere with or get in the way of the child's learning. Many of the problems observed in children with learning disabilities are listed, with illustrative examples given. Suggestions for working around the problems, as well as improving performance, are given. Trial-and-error will help locate the best suggestion for a particular child. Don't forget to stop using these "crutches" as soon as possible. Don't cripple the child by continuing to "help" him when he is strong enough to begin coping with his environment.

Visual Distractibility

The visually distractible child notices everything "see-able," whether it is appropriate for him to do so or not. He responds to movement around him, a flickering light, scratches on the desk top, pictures in the reader, and light streaming through the window. He may be a good or poor visual learner; but, whether he gets accurate information from the visual surroundings or not, he notices them and is attracted by them.

Suggestions:

1. Use a study carrel for individual work, but only when needed.

2. Be sure any duplicated material is free of streaks or blotches.

3. Keep the child's desk clear.

4. Minimize the number of items on a page. If workbooks are used, cut-and-paste as necessary to prevent overcorwded pages.

5. Try using a green marker for a "start here" indicator; a red one for "stop."

6. Get desk tops refinished as soon as they get badly marked.

7. Don't paste a number line or name tag on the desk top—put it some place handy, but out of sight.

8. Beware dangly earrings or polka-dot neckties!

9. Seat this child where he has a clear view of the "action," never behind a hyperactive child!

10. Watch for eye contact with this child—if his eyes are elsewhere, his mind may be, too.

11. Put a blank sheet of paper in the child's book. When he reads on one page, the blank page can cover the opposite page. He can also use a blank paper to cover his own written work, line by line, as he completes it.

Auditory Distractibility

This child responds to every sound. A cough or hiccough can distract his attention from what you're saying. A squeaky desk chair can interfere with his written work. Another child's use of a tape recorder or record player may prevent his being able to work his math.

Suggestions:

1. Have his study carrel lined with acoustic tile or carpet remnants.
2. Try having him wear old stereo headphones, or industrial ear-protectors, especially while he's working on difficult seatwork.
3. Avoid jangly jewelry.
4. Get buzzing light fixtures replaced at once.
5. Request classroom carpeting.
6. Oil desk top hinges.

7. Seat him as far as possible from hyperactive children.
8. Have the tape recorder, etc., used by other children, equipped with headphones or used in carrels whenever possible.

Motor Disinhibition

This child reacts to every object which suggests "doing." He can't walk past the pencil sharpener without turning the handle. A pencil in the hand means a line must be drawn; scissors mean something must be cut. Paste must be tasted; and balls must be thrown, bounced, or rolled. A small tear in a piece of paper suggests a bigger tear. Pencils are chewed. Anything within reach is touched or "fiddled-with."

Suggestions:

1. Keep desk tops clear.
2. Give instructions first; then give materials.
3. In individual instructions, try touching the child or holding his hands while talking to him.
4. Hide the pencil sharpener!
5. Put the waste basket far from his desk.
6. Limit the number of objects he uses at any one time.
7. Take up his paper as soon as it's completed, or have a specific place he's to put it.
8. Have "desk-cleanout" at least once a week, so that there is less "junk" to play with when the child should be working.

Emotional Lability

This child has moods. One minute he's jolly; the next he's in tears or in a rage. Little things "bug" him all out of proportion. You never know when he'll be set off.

Suggestions:

1. Try to be emotionally stable yourself!
2. Don't seat two children with this problem together.
3. Keep a schedule, and try to prepare the child for any changes. When deviations from the schedule must occur, arrange to be near this child.
4. Arrange for "talking time," and help the child channel his expressions of emotions.
5. Encourage the child to control his emotions, and praise him for every tough situation he masters.

Hyperactivity

This child may seem to be "climbing the walls." He's in constant motion. He's out of his desk often, and when he's in it, more often than not, he has one foot curled up under him and the other out in the aisle, ready to move again. He wiggles, taps, jiggles, and never walks but always runs.

Suggestions:

1. Alternate quiet and active periods.
2. Keep work periods short at first; lengthen them as the child becomes able to cope.

3. Send him on "bogus" errands when he seems to need to move. If he *must* move, keep it purposeful.

4. Explore behavior modification techniques for helping him learn to maximize his "still" time.

5. When he's still, however briefly, praise him!

Perseveration

The child who perseverates seems to "get stuck" in a particular pattern of behavior and can't stop when appropriate. Asked to draw six circles, he fills the page. His crayons are worn down to tiny nubs, while the pictures he draws with them are thick with color. When he paints, he scrubs the brushes across the paper until he's painting the easel through a big hole in the paper. He may chatter incessantly on an irrelevant theme.

Suggestions:

1. Keep work assignments specific. If he is to draw six circles, put six marks as indicators.

2. Take up work as soon as it is completed.

3. Praise work which is not "over-done," even if you have intervened to prevent perseveration.

4. For verbal perseveration, try specific limits: "You have told me three things about your dog Brownie. You may tell me one more thing, and then it will be Janet's turn."

5. For drill work which may require repetition of a single task, use a variety of approaches: Six circles can be specified as one circle with each of six crayons; a word to be written in different locations on the worksheet.

Short Attention Span

The child who is hyperactive and/or distractible has a short attention span by virtue of his presence or attention being removed from his task; but not all children with short attention spans are hyperactive or distractible. Some children work hard at a task for a while, and then sit in despair or depression, looking at the remaining work as though it were too great a challenge, even when the work is well within their ability. Pushing beyond the attention span limits influences children differently, depending upon any other problems they may have. Tears, rages, hyperactivity, negativism—the possibilities are there. While helping to increase the child's attention span is a must if one of the **educational goals is to return him to the regular classroom**, a gradual approach may be helpful.

Suggestions:

1. Start by eliminating the child's response to the end of his attention span by *preventing* that response: Determine the length of the child's attention span, and change activities *before* he "runs out" of attention. Praise him for "working hard the whole time."

2. Obviously, you'll have to keep assignments short. It may be better to have two or three short periods when the child works on a given subject (with only a few items per page) than one long period.

3. Keep the number of practice items on any skill to the minimum.

4. Put critical items first in any assignment, with drill items last, so that you can interrupt if necessary without cutting off the more important tasks.

5. Watch for early signs of loss of attention. If the child's attention begins to wander, wait *until it returns* to the task; then interrupt with praise: "Hey, you're really working hard on that! Let's take a rest and work on this later." If you wait until attention is too far gone, this won't work!

6. Gradually increase the child's work periods, letting him know how well he's doing: "Chip, did you know you worked for seven minutes on math without looking up once? Great going!"

General Suggestions

Remind yourself that these interference problems are not learning disabilities, but that they can and do get in the way of the child's ability to learn. The best visual learner loses valuable learning time if he's also hyperactive and must be plucked off the ceiling or desk top regularly. If these interfering problems increase in intensity, examine what's happening in your classroom. If home and personal factors may be putting pressure on the child, there may be little you can do about them; you *can*, however, check your classroom routine to see if you're inadvertently putting on too much pressure yourself.

Avoid the temptation to suggest medication to the parents or to the doctor. As a sign in a convenience market reads, "We have an agreement with the bank: They don't sell groceries, and we don't cash checks." Unfortunately, too many teachers and parents *demand* medication of the doctor rather than asking him about it. Some of my medical colleagues have suggested that medication given to control these behaviors frequently associated with learning disabilities, when *unnecessarily* given, may indeed control them, but may completely eliminate the possibility of the child's learning to control his behavior. One chubby, tantruming eight-year-old dramatically illustrates this danger: As he flung himself, kicking and screaming, to the floor, he skrieked at his teacher, "You know I can't control myself! I didn't have my medication today."

Many children, however, are helped immeasurably by medication. The danger comes when medication is given indiscriminately, or because parents or teachers have tried to take over the physician's role in deciding whether or not it is indicated in a particular case.

In all areas, both academic and behavioral, the goal should be to help the child develop as many techniques for dealing with his problems as can be devised, to avoid making him dependent on extensive special material or outside controls, and to normalize his education as much as possible.

The child is best served when each of the professionals helping him works at his or her own job. Usually, no one can do your job as well as you can. If you waste your time taking over someone else's role, you no longer have that time to spend on your unique part in helping.

Chapter 7

Individualizing Learning In Groups: Simple Behavior Modification

The regular classroom teacher, asking to consider yet another aspect of individual differences, is likely to throw up her hands in dismay. She has thirty students, working on many levels, with varied personalities, interests, and motivational levels. Here, she has been asked to consider not only the learner's ability, but his style as well.

How can the teacher manage to maintain order and deal with the many varied facets of classroom individualization? Obviously, careful planning is a must. But beyond the most careful planning and the most complete, individual plans, the teacher must still be able to observe and assist; to teach one or a group of students while others continue their work. The biggest problem, most teachers say, is not in the planning and individualizing, but in maintaining order while freeing the teacher to teach.

"I wanted to be a teacher, not a policeman!" agonizes the teacher. (See illustration on following page.)

Psychological research, in seeking solutions to severe behavioral problems, resulted in laboratory solutions which worked with people, just as they had worked with pigeons, rats, and other laboratory animals. Psychologists began to suggest to teachers that they might try these approaches with their classrooms. Many teachers resisted—and still do resist—these approaches. Called operant conditioning or behavior modification, precision teaching or contingency contracting, there was still too much of a flavor of bribery or "mind control" to appeal to teachers. And besides, many teachers said, those white-coated psychologists are working one-to-one in a clinical setting, maybe for a hour a couple of times a week. "I have *thirty* kids, six hours a day, five days a week. How am I supposed to keep thirty different jelly bean schedules? And what do I do with the mothers yelling about the increased dental bills from so many jelly beans?"

Sometimes, behavior modification people tend to talk as though their approaches were a new invention rather than a discovery of a set of principles underlying behavior. A young psychologist might suggest "placing on extinction" certain attention-seeking behavior in fourth-grade boys. The teacher with years of experience already knows that the best way to get rid of such behavior is to ignore it. It's the same principle at work—they're just using different words for it!

There has been truth on both sides of the controversy. Often, the behavior modifier has been wrong—some behaviors *can't* wait while the teacher makes observations, counting how many times per day or per hour the behavior occurs. Often, the teacher has been wrong, too. Having a child work for a reward, rather than "because it's good for him" is no more bribery than paying that same teacher a salary.

It is not the purpose of this book to train teachers in behavior modification. It is a rare teacher indeed who has not had graduate or undergraduate course, or in-service training in behavior modification! Before reviewing the suggestions given here however, the teacher would do well to review the basic principles, either in her own class or through in-service notes, or in one of the basic behavior modification books listed in the bibliography.

Here is a "baker's dozen" of behavior modification hints which may get you started in looking at behavior, and your responses to it, in a new way:

1. Where behavior is concerned, "you've got to know one to change one."

For example:

Statement: "Johnny won't behave!"
Question: "What does he do?"
Answer: "Well, oh, he's always cutting up."
Solution: "Take away his scissors!"
Statement: "That's *not* what I meant!"

2. If a stranger can't count or measure the behavior by your definition, better redefine it!

No: "Sally misbehaves."
Yes: "Sally gets out of her seat, hits other children, and speaks out without raising her hand."

Poor Terms: misbehaving
bothering others
doing nothing
Better Terms: getting out of seat
touching or hitting others
looking out the window

3. Be sure your reward is rewarding!

    Is a grade of "B" a reward?

        To a "C" student?

        To an "A" student?

    Is a dime for candy rewarding?

        To a kid with a painful cavity?

        To a kid who gets $5 a week allowance?

4. Be sure the students know the rules!

    "But, officer, I didn't know the speed limit was 55!"

5. Be sure the rules are abide-by-able!

    No matter *how* strong the reward is, your cat won't recite the Gettysburg Address, a retarded child won't do calculus, and a hyperactive child simply may not be able to sit still for half an hour.

6. Change your way of stating things!

    Don't say these:

    "Well, OK, you can color now if you promise to do your math later."

    "No, you can't go out until you finish your homework.

    Say these instead:

    "Yes, you may color, just as soon as you've done your math."

    "Yes, you can go out as soon as you finish your homework."

7. Reward *every time* to get a good thing started. Reward *occasionally* to keep them going and make them last.

8. Behavior doesn't exist in a vacuum or "Idle hands are the devil's workshop."

    Example:

    If you don't want Tommy to beat up on George, decide what you *do* want him to do, and tell him to do it. Then reward him!

Don't say:

"I don't know why I should go out of my way to drive you downtown. You *know* you're supposed to pick up your dirty clothes! etc. etc."

Say instead:

"Oh, Cindy, get those dirty clothes in the hamper, will you?"
Pause
"Looks great now! Ready for that ride to town?"

9. What's it worth to you?

Behavior "mod" takes time, planning, and even, sometimes, a little pocket change. But would you be willing to spend fifteen minutes reading a story, or maybe two minutes (and 89 ¢ !) giving out gumdrops or peanuts if it meant 26 kids *cheerfully* did three pages of math each?

10. Old behaviors that used to get results are the hardest to get rid of, even if they don't work any more!

Example:

On the first few nights after you institute a "bedtime's 8:00 no matter *what* that kid does" rule, expect a long, hard time of it. After all, if five mintues of howling worked last night, won't he want to find out if maybe tonight you just didn't hear? So he'll howl longer, and louder . . . !

11. New behavior that doesn't get prompt results goes away.

Example:

Why do so many reducing diets fall by the wayside?

Example:

It works the other way, too. The class clown who's ignored by his peers soon gets quiet.

12. Restate the rule often. It's a reminder; and it lets the behavior, not you or the child, be the "bad guy."

For example:

No: "No, son, you didn't eat your vegetables, so you can't have chocolate pudding."

No: "Better hurry up and eat those vegetables, or no chocolate pudding for you!"

Yes: "The rule is: When you've eaten all your dinner, you may have dessert."

Yes: "Better hurry up and eat those vegetables, so you can have chocolate pudding!"

13. Avoid punishment at all costs!

It *may* cause the "punishee" to avoid the punisher, instead of avoiding the behavior! Ever notice how the punitive teacher's class goes *wild* when she's called to the office unexpectedly?

Perhaps the area where disagreement has caused the most difficulty is in the issue of managing a large group of children so that each learns. The teacher wants some technique that's easy to administer and frees her to teach. The behavior modifier understands *individual* behavior modification systems that control disruptive behavior or reward achievement. And if 15 children are working on 12 different things, that's difficult.

One deceptively simple way which *does* work requires almost no extra work once it is set up by the teacher. It results in more freedom for the teacher to teach. Students who have been involved in this approach for one class period a day often ask their teachers to use it throughout the day! It's a group approach which requires each student to be "on task" throughout a set period of time. And the only equipment required is a simple bell-type kitchen timer.

Setting up a group behavior modification system is perhaps one of the easiest processes possible. First, you have to decide exactly what behaviors constitute being "on task." This may vary widely from one teacher to another. For example, you may feel that it is perfectly appropriate for a child to get up quietly and sharpen his pencil when necessary, or ask a friend for a piece of paper. Another teacher may not want any talking or any out-of-seat behavior without hand raising and permission granted. Those decisions become part of the set of rules, spoken or unspoken, that each teacher establishes.

Experiences behavior modifiers insist that you need to find out exactly how the situation stacks up *before* you begin the project. This is "getting baseline data," and is often the most frustrating aspect of behavior modification for teachers, who see a problem *now* and want to start solving it *now*. Whenever possible, though, it is best to get baseline information. If nothing else, you can delight in your later success in black-and-white, not just a "feeling" that it's working.

The best—and perhaps only—way to get baseline data for the group approach is to get help from someone else. A teacher's aide, a supervisor, or perhaps an interested parent, can be a willing helper.

Carefully go over the rules you've decided on with your helper. Be sure you both interpret the rules the same way.

For example, suppose your only rules are:

1. Raise your hand for permission to talk.
2. Raise your hand for permission to leave your desk.

In that case, these two children are following the rules and are on task:

1. Mary Sue, who's gazing out the window.
2. Tom, who's waving his arms wildly to get your attention.

The following children are *not* on task:

1. Ralph, going quietly to the pencil sharpener without permission.
2. Cindy, quietly asking Marsha for a piece of paper.

In other words, your rules must suit the kind of atmosphere you want in your classroom, be specific enough so that they cover the situations you may encounter, and be simple enough so that the students can keep up with them.

Once you and your helper understand what "on task" means in your classroom, you're ready to collect data. One way to get a good cross-section is to observe each child in turn for a brief interval—say, three or five seconds—and record just whether he's on task or off task, according to your definitions. (That fast timing takes a little practice, but is easier than you might think!) Continue to observe each child in turn until your observation covers a set period, such as fifteen minutes. You can make up a simple form, like Figure F, to make your observations simpler. This way, your observer simply glances at each child, makes a

Figure F

CLASSROOM OBSERVATION CHECKLIST

Classroom _____ Date _____

Teacher _____ Observer _____

Activity _____

Time Begun _____ Time Ended _____

Name	1	2	3	4	5	6	7	8	9	10
	+/−	+/−	+/−	+/−	+/−	+/−	+/−	+/−	+/−	+/−
	+/−	+/−	+/−	+/−	+/−	+/−	+/−	+/−	+/−	+/−
	+/−	+/−	+/−	+/−	+/−	+/−	+/−	+/−	+/−	+/−
	+/−	+/−	+/−	+/−	+/−	+/−	+/−	+/−	+/−	+/−
	+/−	+/−	+/−	+/−	+/−	+/−	+/−	+/−	+/−	+/−
	+/−	+/−	+/−	+/−	+/−	+/−	+/−	+/−	+/−	+/−
	+/−	+/−	+/−	+/−	+/−	+/−	+/−	+/−	+/−	+/−

decision as to whether teh child is on task or off task, and marks the appropriate response with a slash through the plus or minus sign.

The observation chart is easy to calculate if you set it up like Figure F. The blanks for the names are in groups of ten, and there are ten columns marked "+ —." If you are observing more children than there are lines on a page, just use two sheets. A clipboard works nicely.

To get your results, simply count by rows of tens how many individual observations were made, and then how many of those observations were on task. (If you've got a pretty well-behaved group, it's easier to count those few off-task times and subtract from the total!) Then calculate the percentage of time on task by dividing the on-task number by the total, and multiplying by hundred. Now you have a measure of how well your class followed the rules for that period. You can also check for individual students having problems staying on task by reading the *rows* of marks by each name.

You'll want to take data on a couple of occasions to get a good overall picture. You should have these observations made during the type of activity you intend to begin the project in, such as a twenty-five-minute math period, or perhaps a half-hour individual work period. As you can see, this method can be used in any situation where your rules are in effect, whether the students are doing quiet work, having class discussion, or working in small groups.

After you have completed your data gathering, you'll need to decide what kind of reward you want to have. Some excellent rewards include free time, listening to records, "talking time," or an extra few minutes added to recess. A reward of time need not be long—an extra four or five mintues to play, or time to play a "rock" record of the group's choice can be a very desirable reward. If in doubt, ask the students. (Behavior modification doesn't *always* have to involve candy rewards!)

Next, look at the period of time you're going to use for your project. Let's say you've decided to use a thirty-minute math period. So that the reward won't be unattainable, you might decide that the students can earn one minute extra recess for each five minutes of on-task time.

Now you're ready to introduce the project to the students. Review the rules carefully—prehaps you'll want the students to give examples. (A good idea is to post the rules conspicuously, and have them read before each session.) Explain what the reward will be, and show your handy kitchen timer to the students. Explain that you'll set the timer for five minutes. As long as everyone is on task, the timer runs. When the bell rings, you'll put one "hash mark" on the board, reset the timer, and continue the lesson. If, however, anyone "messes up" and breaks a rule, you will reset the timer to five minutes—even if it has almost run down!

Keep in mind that *the system* is going to work on the behavior. If someone breaks a rule—speaks out of turn, for example—it's important that you merely reset the timer *without comment or facial grimace*! Just keep right on with the lesson.

At first, when one student breaks a rule and the timer is reset, other students may berate the rule-breaker—thus breaking the rules themselves. When this happens, just make a poker-faced show of picking up the timer again and resetting—even if it hasn't really started to run down. If you feel it's necessary, you can explain that berating rule-breakers is taboo. You might mention it briefly during the rule review just before your next session, but then drop it, and use the timer instead. Disruption of the "Oh, no, you messed it up for all of us" type disappears quickly! Within a very few sessions, you'll have very high percentage of on-task behavior. (Be sure to have your helper take data again, so you can brag about your class's improvement!) Later, you may want to try working on longer class periods, longer time intervals (seven to ten minutes). You can very soon turn the timer duty over to a student. Frequently, this works even better. After using the system, some teachers find themselves relenting too much on the rules ("Well, he started to talk out, but stopped after two words.") and weakening their system. Using students as timekeepers usually eliminates this problem—they're firm, but fair!

The younger the student, the sooner you'll have to give the reward. For example, you may want to give that free time immediately aftre the work period. Older students often enjoy saving it up for fun class activities, like a popcorn party or field trip.

83

Once this system is in effect, you can use it for any classroom situations, freeing yourself for individual work as needed. The students learn to be responsible for their own behavior, and many "reformed rowdies" comment on how enjoyable it is to be able to work in peace and quiet!

Behavior modification isn't magic, or bribery, or a cure-all. It is an effective system which can't accomplish anything alone. Good curriculum, good methods, and good material are still critical if the students are to learn. Behavior modification is merely one tool at the teacher's command which can help her implement a well-organized, appropriate program for the students.

Conclusion

    Perhaps you're an "old hand" in learning disabilities, and you've been a teacher or parent of learning-disabled kids for quite some time. If so, you will have found here many **suggestions** you've known and used as long as you can remember. Maybe, though, I've given you one or two new ideas you can use. And maybe you can send me some of your hints that others can share!

    Perhaps, on the other hand, learning disabilities is a new area to you as a parent or teacher. If so, I hope I've cleared up a few mysteries and given you some practical suggestions you can use *right now*. Don't stop here, though! There are many books—more thorough, deeper, and there'll be some newer—which can expand your knowledge and expertise. Then you'll soon be one of those "old hands" who know at least a dozen good ideas, and even better ones, for each one I've given here. Then you can share some of your ideas with us, too!

Suggested Readings

The following books are more thorough texts on learning disabilities. Most of them include a basic section of definitions of learning disabilities: history, theory, and diagnostic materials, followed by a section on activities and strategies for remediation.

Bangs, Tina. *Language and Learning Disorders of Pre-Academic Children.* New York: Appleton-Century-Crofts, 1968.

Cruickshank, William M. *The Brain-Injured Child in Home, School and Community.* Syracuse, New York: Syracuse University Press, 1967.

Frierson, Edward C. and Barbe, Walter B. *Educating Children with Learning Disabilities:* Selected Readings. New York: Appleton-Century-Crofts, 1961.

Hallahan, Daniel P. and Cruickshank, William M. *Psycho-Educational Foundations of Learning Disabilities.* Englewood Cliffs, New Jersey: Prentice-Hall, 1973.

Hammill, Donald D. and Bartel, Nettie R. *Educational Perspectives in Learning Disabilities.* New York: John Wiley and Sons, 1971.

Hammill, Donald D. and Bartel, Nettie R. *Teaching Children with Learning Disabilities.* Boston: Allyn and Bacon, 1975.

Johnson Doris J. and Myklebust, Helmer. *Learning Disabilities: Education Principles and Practices.* New York: Grune and Stratton, 1967.

Kephart, Newell C. *The Slow Learner in the Classroom* (second ed). Columbus, Ohio: Charles E. Merrill, 1971.

Lerner, Janet W. *Children with Learning Disabilities.* Boston: Houghton Mifflin, 1971.

McCarthy, James J. and McCarthy, Joan F. *Learning Disabilities.* Boston: Allyn and Bacon, 1969.

Myers, Patricia and Hammill, Donald D. *Methods for Learning Disorders.* New York: John Wiley and Sons, 1969.

Myklebust, Helmer R. and Johnson, Doris J. *Learning Disabilities.* New York: Grune and Stratton, 1968.

Myklebust, Helmer R. *Progress in Learning Disabilities,* Volume I. New York: Grune and Stratton, 1968.

Wallace, Gerald and Kauffman, James M. *Teaching Children with Learning Problems.* Columbus, Ohio: Charles E. Merrill, 1973.

Wallace, Gerald and McLoughlin, James A. *Learning Disabilities: Concepts and Characteristics.* Columbus, Ohio: Charles E. Merrill, 1975.

These books are almost entirely "how-to" books, full of remedial activities.

Arena, John I. (ed). *Teaching Through Sensory-Motor Experiences.* Belmont, California: Academic Therapy Publications, in association with Fearon Publishers, 1969.

Behrmann, Polly. *Activities for Developing Visual Perception.* San Rafael, California: Academic Therapy Publications, 1970.

Behrmann, Polly. *How Many Spoons Make A Family?* San Rafael, California: Academic Therapy Publications, 1971.

Bush, Wilma J. and Giles, Marian Taylor. *Aids to Psycholinguistic Teaching.* Columbus, Ohio: Charles E. Merrill, 1969.

Frostig, Marianne and Maslow, Phyllis. *Learning Problems in the Classroom.* New York: Grunne and Stratton, 1973.

Mallison, Ruth. *Education as Therapy.* Seattle: Special Child Publications, 1968.

Murphy, Patricia. *A Special Way for the Special Child in the Regular Classroom.* San Rafael, California: Academic Therapy Publications, 1971.

Smith, Robert M. *Teacher Diagnosis of Educational Difficulties.* Columbus, Ohio: Charles E. Merrill, 1969.

The following are practical guides to behavior modification techniques. They are useful for both parents and teachers.

Becker, Wesley C. *Parents Are Teachers.* Champaign, Illinois: Research Press, 1971.

Canter, Lee. *The Whys & Hows of Working with Behavior Problems in the Classroom.* San Rafael, California: Academic Therapy Publications, 1974.

Krumboltz, John D. and Krumboltz, Helen Brandhorst. *Changing Children's Behavior.* Englewood Cliffs, New Jersey: Prentice-Hall, 1972.

Patterson, Gerald R. and Gullion, M. Elizabeth. *Living with Children.* Champaign, Illinois: Research Press, 1968.

White, Thelma D. *My Mom Uses Behavior Modification.* Grove City, Ohio: South-Western City Schools, 1972.

Zifferblatt, Steven M. *You Can Help Your Child Improve Study and Homework Behaviors.* Champaign, Illinois: Research Press, 1970.